Contents

UNIT 1

UNIT 2

UNIT 3

SPECIAL NOTE

The following additional resources are available on the CD-ROM:

Unit 3.19 – Add, load, show and hide multiple forms

Unit 3.20 – File system objects: drive, directory and file list boxes

Unit 3.21 – Databases: finding, adding and deleting data

Unit 3.22 – Working with text files

Unit 3.23 – For Each … Next: checkboxes, tags and the controls collection

Unit 3.24 – Using control arrays

UNIT 4

Unit 4.1 – Plan your projects

Unit 4.2 – How to tackle projects

Using a structure diagram

Using procedures

To be able to use the programs and practise the coded examples, you will need a copy of Microsoft® Visual Basic® 6 which was used to produce the materials. Earlier versions of Microsoft® Visual Basic®, such as 4 and 5, could also be used.

Introduction

This book has been written as a resource for the delivery of the programming element in the Standard Grade Computing Studies syllabus. It introduces programming concepts in the Microsoft® Visual Basic® for Windows® programming environment. Programming is at the heart of Computing and Microsoft® Visual Basic® has the capacity to engage the novice programmer with its familiar Windows graphical-user interface and event-driven context.

The book is intended for use within the period of the two-year Standard Grade Computing Studies course. It consists of four units, which take you progressively through the various levels at Standard Grade. Unit 1 is aimed at the Foundation level with Units 2 and 3 allowing progression to General and Credit levels. The latter chapters of Unit 3 (included on the CD-ROM) are intended as extension material for enthusiastic Credit level students or those intending to go on to the Higher Still. Unit 4 on the CD-ROM provides useful guidance to students preparing programming projects for assessment by giving detailed design tips.

Each topic in the book begins with an exemplar project that you are encouraged to work through as practice material. The "Now you try" sections come after each topic and allow you to try out the new concepts you have learned. At the end of some sections "Supertasks" are provided to challenge you and test your knowledge and ability.

Although the book has been written with the Scottish Standard Grade in mind it is suitable for any general introductory course in programming or for the individual programming enthusiast.

Resources

A CD-ROM is supplied with the book and is integral for the completion of exemplar tasks. It also contains additional resources for Unit 3 and Unit 4. It is divided into four sections:

- **Unit 2 and Unit 3**: These two sections contain programming examples and image libraries that support their respective sections either in the book or in the Additional Resources section on the CD-ROM.
- **Additional Resources**: This section contains additional material for Unit 3 and Unit 4, which contains information about project planning.
- **Unit 4**: This section contains examples and structure diagrams to support Unit 4 in the Additional Resources section on the CD-ROM.

A note for students

If you are new to programming and want to learn programming, or you need to produce programs using Microsoft® Windows® for your Computing course, then this book is for you. This programming book is intended to introduce you to Microsoft® Visual Basic® which will allow you to create fully functioning Microsoft® Windows® programs with the minimum of effort.

Microsoft® Visual Basic® is an event-driven programming language, which means that you can easily produce windows (forms) so that the user can interact with your program. Producing these windows does not require complicated programming code; they can be easily drawn with the sophisticated tools provided. So if you can use a mouse and keyboard and are familiar with using Microsoft® Windows®, then you will have no problem in creating the user's interface.

Creating the user interface, important as it is, is only the beginning. You will be required to write program instructions in the Microsoft® Visual Basic® programming language. The language, however, is easy to learn and is very powerful and you will quickly master how to carry out programming tasks.

If you are new to Microsoft® Visual Basic® or to programming in general, you should start at the beginning of the book and work your way through the tasks. Each topic section begins with an exemplar programming problem. You should use the Microsoft® Visual Basic® "Integrated Programming Environment" (IDE) to create the forms and type in code. Take your time to produce the exemplar tasks so that subsequently you can use the new concepts and skills learned to tackle the "Now you try" problems and the "Supertasks". Also take time to read Unit 4 on the CD-ROM as it will help you in producing and submitting projects for assessment purposes.

The demonstration projects and procedures provided on the CD-ROM, as well as allowing you to carry out more complex tasks, will also, if you care to browse the coding involved, show you how more demanding problems can be solved.

While you are developing your projects in the IDE you can run and debug your programs in the interpreted mode. Whenever you feel that your program is complete you can compile it from the **File** menu and create an executable version (.exe). This will allow you to distribute your program without the requirement that your users have Microsoft® Visual Basic® on their computers.

I have not been able to include everything about Microsoft® Visual Basic® in this book since it is a vast and complex environment and would require a much larger volume than allowed by this short introduction. However, if you master the concepts and skills it provides in these units, you will be well on your way to producing sophisticated and useful projects.

I hope you enjoy using this programming guide and have fun in producing the tasks set and creating your own Microsoft® Visual Basic® programs. Good luck!

Abe Holmes

Running the CD-ROM

Note: You may be required to restart your PC after running the CD-ROM for the first time.

• Insert the CD into your CD-ROM drive, and it should run automatically.

If your PC does not support autorun:

• Go to **My Computer** and double-click on your CD-ROM drive. The CD-ROM should run.

If it does not run, but instead displays a list of the files on the CD-ROM, then double-click on the file *start.exe*.

While using the CD-ROM, click on the question mark to obtain help on how the CD-ROM works and how to access the files you want to use.

UNIT 1

1.1 Getting started

Introducing Visual Basic

In this book you will learn to program using Visual Basic for Windows. Visual Basic is a very popular programming language because it allows you to create useful programs that work with the Windows operating system.

When you program for Windows the visual impact of your program is important, so you need to learn how to use objects like **buttons**, **labels**, **text boxes** and **list boxes** that come with Visual Basic. You can create programs very quickly by placing these objects on a form – see Figure 1.1.

In order to make things easy for you Visual Basic comes with a **Toolbox**. The Toolbox holds the objects that can be selected and then drawn onto the form – see Figure 1.2.

Later you will be shown, step by step, how to create the objects on the form. In Figure 1.3 you can see that two buttons and a list box have been placed on the form.

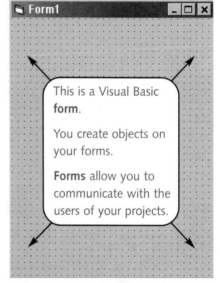

This is a Visual Basic **form**.

You create objects on your forms.

Forms allow you to communicate with the users of your projects.

Figure 1.1 A Visual Basic form

Figure 1.2
The Visual Basic Toolbox

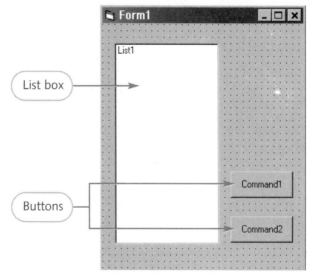

Figure 1.3 A Visual Basic form with buttons and a list box

However, just by placing these objects on a form does not make a finished Visual Basic program. You have to write instructions that will respond to an action a user of the program might perform. The user might click on a button, for example, so Visual Basic will have to react to this **event**. What happens next depends on what instructions you wrote into the button.

Let's say that you want the list box to be filled with a *list of names* as soon as the user clicks the button. The instructions on the button will have to do just that. You will see how to do that when you create your first program in the next chapter.

Jargon buster

Program – A set of instructions that is carried out by the computer's processor.

Operating system – A special program that allows the computer to be used. For example, Windows 2000 and XP are operating systems.

Running Visual Basic

When Visual Basic was installed on your computer certain **icons** and **menu items** were created on your system. Here are two ways to start Visual Basic.

If a **folder** for Visual Basic is visible on your Desktop, open the folder and click the Visual Basic icon to run the program – see Figure 1.4.

Figure 1.4 How the Visual Basic folder might look

Another way to start the program is to click on the Windows **Start button** to reveal Programs ▶ Microsoft Visual Basic 6.0. Select Visual Basic 6.0, as in Figure 1.5.

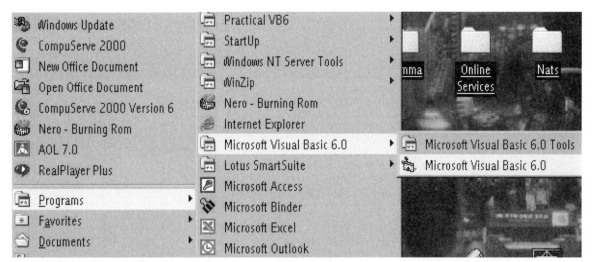

Figure 1.5 Opening Visual Basic from the Start cascading menus

When you have succeeded in launching Visual Basic the **New Project** window will appear, as in Figure 1.6. When you are ready to start a new project, click on **Open** because the **Standard.exe icon** is selected by default, as in the screenshot.

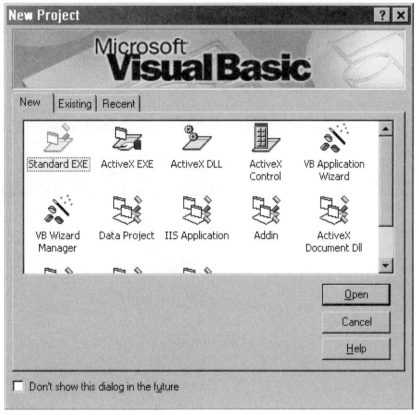

Figure 1.6 The New Project window

When you start the new project Visual Basic automatically creates a new form for you. Visual Basic gives it the name **Form1**. Look at Figure 1.7 on the next page to see how a new project has been created and a new form called *Form1* is already visible. Notice also the *Toolbox* to the left of Form1.

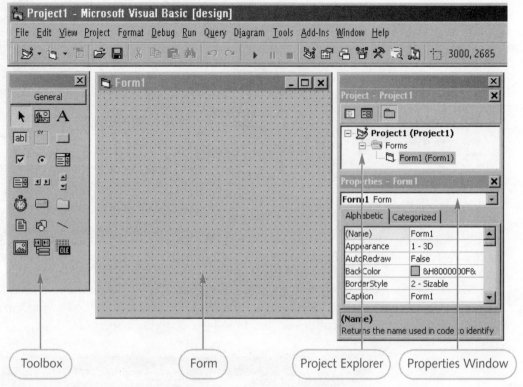

Figure 1.7 Visual Basic has started with a new form, called **Form1**

Making the form visible

What happens if you cannot see your form? Try these tips:

- click this **icon** on the Toolbar and then double-click the **form icon** in the
  Project Explorer

- *or* from the **View** menu select Project Explorer and double-click the **form icon** in the
  Project Explorer – see Figure 1.8.

Figure 1.8
Making your form visible

Making the Toolbox visible

What happens if you cannot see the Toolbox? Try these tips:

- click this **icon** on the toolbar

- *or* from the **View** menu select Toolbox.

When we have looked at the **Project Explorer** and the **Properties Window** you can start placing objects on the form. Let's first look at the Project Explorer.

The Project Explorer

When the Project Explorer window becomes visible it will display any forms that the project already contains.

Sometimes the Project Explorer becomes hidden. You can always get it back by either:

- clicking this **icon** on the toolbar

- *or* by selecting Project Explorer from the **View** menu
- *or* by using the keystrokes **Ctrl + R**.

If you have *saved* the project it will also display the filenames you used for the forms and project.

The Properties Window

In many of the projects you create you will have to change the **properties** of the **objects** on the form. You will learn more about this in detail later.

To make sure the Properties Window is displayed for an object, press **F4** *when the object is selected*.

Two more ways to make the Properties Window visible are:

- select Properties Window from the **View** menu
- *or* click this icon on the **Toolbar**.

Jargon buster

Running – When applied to a computer program, *running* means that the processor is carrying out the instructions that have been written into the program at design time.

Standard.exe – This option allows you to create a program that you can later turn into an *executable file* that can run on any computer with Windows, without the need to have Visual Basic installed.

Project – Although the word *program* is usually adequate to describe what you are creating, because of the visual nature of Visual Basic the word *project* better describes all the components that a Visual Basic program contains.

Property – *Objects* in Visual Basic can be altered both in appearance and how they behave. To change an object's appearance and behaviour you have to set its properties. For example a *button* has a *caption* property.

Creating objects on the form

Now that you have Visual Basic running it's time to learn how to create **objects** on the form. Follow the step-by-step instructions below to place **buttons** and a **list box** onto **Form1** using the **Toolbox**.

When you click a **control** on the Toolbox in Visual Basic and then move over to the form, the pointer will change to a **crosshair** (like a plus sign). Drag across the form to make the control the size you want it to be.

Creating a command button

1 Click on the **command button control** (arrowed in Figure 1.9).

2 Move over to the form and drag out a button **shape**. Adjust the **size** of the button by using the handles that appear around the button when it is selected.

3 To create more buttons, simply repeat steps 1 and 2.

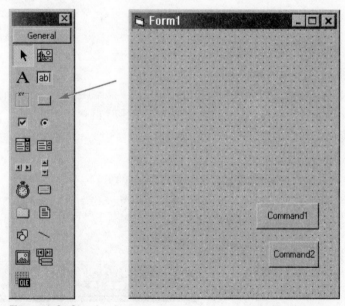

Figure 1.9 Creating buttons

In Figure 1.9, two command buttons have been created.

The same steps are involved when you create other objects, such as **labels**, **list boxes**, **text boxes**, and **image and picture frames**.

Creating a list box

If you double-click the control creation tool on the Toolbox the object will automatically be placed in the middle of the current active form. You can then size and place the object where you want.

On the form in Figure 1.10 a list box has been created by this method and is selected for sizing or being moved to another position. You will often need to move and size objects after you have placed them on the form.

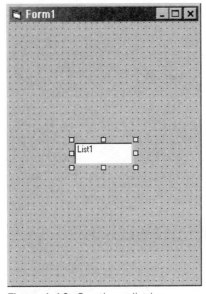

Figure 1.10 Creating a list box

Moving an object

1 Click on the object you want to move, to select it.

2 Drag the object with the mouse and reposition it where you want.

Sizing an object

1 Click on the object you want to size to select it and reveal its **sizing handles**.

2 Click and drag on one of the handles to allow you to increase or decrease the size of the object.

3 If you want to increase the length and height of the object at the same time, use one of the **corner handles**.

Changing the size of the form

1 Move the mouse to the edge of the form.

2 When the cursor changes to a **two-headed arrow** drag to size the form.

Creating a list box and command buttons

Our first Visual Basic program will be to get the computer to display a list of names in a list box. Being able to display information is a very important part of most computer programs.

In the previous chapter you were shown how to open a form and create the objects you will need for this simple program. You are going to need two buttons and a list box.

The list box object in Visual Basic is used to display information as a table. Remember that you can place the list box anywhere you like on the form.

- One of the buttons will allow the user to click and get Visual Basic to display a list of names. What the names are does not really matter, but they could be a team list for example.

- The other button will have the simple task of stopping the program when the user decides to click it.

Always begin a Visual Basic project by planning what your form is going to look like for the user. This involves drawing out a form on paper, including the objects that you propose to use. Also label what the objects are meant to be and what their purpose is, as in Figure 1.11.

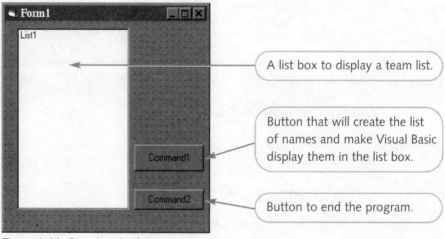

Figure 1.11 Planning the form

It can also be useful to write down what you plan to do:

- *Create one list box.* This will display a team list.
- *Create two buttons.* One will create the list in the list box and the other will stop the program.

OK, so that's the plan. You should now try to create the form and the objects by carrying out the step-by-step instructions that follow.

Creating the form

Run Visual Basic so that you have a new project ready. Make sure that the Toolbox is visible. If it is not visible go to the **View** menu and choose **Toolbox**. Size the form to about 8cm square, as you learned in the previous chapter.

Creating the list box

Create a list box on Form1 by using the **ListBox** control (see Figure 1.12). Visual Basic calls it **List1**.

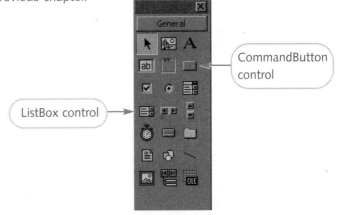

ListBox control

CommandButton control

Figure 1.12 Select a control from the Toolbox

After you click a control on the Toolbox, move over to the form and the pointer will change to a crosshair (+). Drag across the form to make the object the size you want. Use the moving and sizing skills you have learned to place the list box as you see in Figure 1.13.

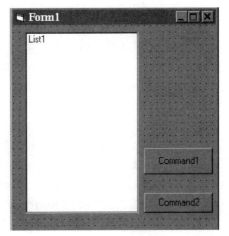

Figure 1.13 The list box has been placed and resized

Jargon buster

Control – In Visual Basic the word *control* means the tool that is used to create the object on the form. It is not unusual for Visual Basic programmers to use the same term to describe the object as well. Controls in the Toolbox are actually programs to allow you to create objects.

Crosshair – The cursor that appears when you are using a control to draw an object on the form.

Creating the buttons

Create two buttons using the **CommandButton** control (Figure 1.12). As with the form, click the control on the Toolbox and move over to the form. Again the pointer will change to a crosshair (+). Drag across the form to create the object the size you want. Repeat the procedure for the second button. Visual Basic calls these buttons **Command1** and **Command2**.

That completes the creation of the form and the objects that we want on it.

Planning the program

A program needs **instructions** to be carried out in order that Visual Basic can do something useful. We have already decided that this program will have a button that when clicked will create a list of names in the list box. The other button will tell Visual Basic to end the program.

Just as you planned the form, always plan the instructions that a program will contain. Let's write down exactly what we want Visual Basic to do.

Plan for the Command1 button

- First of all clear the list box. Use the **List1.Clear** instruction to do this.
- Then add a list of names to List1, using the **List1.AddItem** instruction for each name in the list.

So the actual Visual Basic instructions for the Command1 button will be:

```
List1.Clear
List1.AddItem "Marcos"
List1.AddItem "Cafu"
List1.AddItem "Roberto Carlos"
List1.AddItem "Kleberson"
List1.AddItem "Gilberto Silva"
List1.AddItem "Lucio"
List1.AddItem "Ronaldo"
List1.AddItem "Rivaldo"
List1.AddItem "Ronaldinho"
List1.AddItem "Edmilson"
List1.AddItem "Roque Junior"
List1.AddItem "Juninho"
List1.AddItem "Denilson"
```

Plan for the Command2 button

- Command2 button will end the program
- The instruction for the Command2 button will be **End**.

Jargon buster

AddItem – When a control is created for the Toolbox, the developer decides what the control will be able to do and how it will be possible to use it. The control is given *methods* that can be applied to it by programmers like you and me. *AddItem* is a method that can be applied to a list box that allows an item to be added to it, for example **List1.AddItem "Shut that door!"**.

Clear – A method that can be applied to a list box to clear its contents at the start of runtime. An example is **List1.Clear**.

Placing the instructions for the buttons

The instructions for both buttons must be placed within the buttons themselves. So let's do that now, starting with the Command1 button.

Command1 button

Double-click the Command1 button object to open its code window. Figure 1.14 shows the code window for the Command1 button with its **click event** visible.

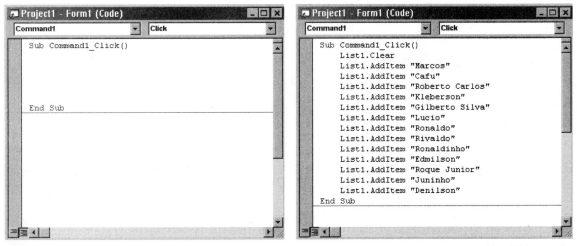

Figure 1.14 How the code window looks on opening, and how it will look after you have typed in the instructions

Next type the list of instructions into the code window, between the two lines that are already there. You must press **Enter** after each line before typing the next one.

When you have finished typing in the instructions into the code window for this button, close it by clicking on the window's close button.

Command2 button

As before, double-click the Command2 button to open its code window. Type the single command that is needed for the Command2 button between the two original lines, as in Figure 1.15. The instruction is **End**.

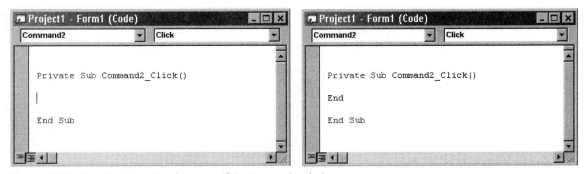

Figure 1.15 Type **End** into the Command2 button code window

As before, when you have finished typing this instruction into the code window for this button, close it by clicking on the window's close button. You are now ready to run the program and test how it performs!

Jargon buster

Event – An event (or an event procedure) is a set of instructions that can be carried out when an object on the form receives an action from the user. The action could be a mouse click for example. For our button called *Command1*, its click event will run the instructions in its **Command1_Click ( )** event procedure.

Running the program

To run a Visual Basic program you need to press **F5** on the keyboard.

Check that your program will run by pressing F5. The program should run and then wait for you to do something. That is because Visual Basic is an **event-driven language**, which means that nothing will happen (apart from the program loading) until it is given an action to carry out by the user.

Jargon buster

Event-driven – A language that is *event-driven* means that processing is driven by events that the user initiates by actions like, for example, clicking on objects.

Testing the program

Now check that the program does what it is supposed to do in response to events.

1 Click the **Command1** button and the list of names should appear in the list box, as in Figure 1.16.

2 Click the **Command2** button and the program will stop running.

You will know that your program has stopped running because the list box will not now be displaying the list of names. You should also see that the **Toolbox**, **Project Explorer** and **Properties Window** will again be visible. When your program is running these are not visible.

If you got that to work, well done! You have created your first Visual Basic project.

Figure 1.16 Good! My program has worked!

Help

Programs don't always work first time. If when you try to run your program it comes up with an error message, you will have to fix the error and try running the program again. First stop your program by going to the **Run** menu and selecting **End**.

If your program does not work it is probable that you have made a mistake in one of the instructions you typed into one of the buttons. Carry out the following steps to correct your program.

1 If there is still an error message on the screen (as in Figure 1.17), click **OK** to get rid of it.

Figure 1.17 Visual Basic notifies you of an error

2 Visual Basic will show you where the problem lies (as in Figure 1.18). Visual Basic cannot continue processing your instructions in the button Command1 because it has encountered this error. Notice that Visual Basic highlights the name of the event where the error is located and the error itself – in this case it is *OddItem* instead of *AddItem*. Because the instruction has been misspelled Visual Basic does not understand what it has to do. This is known as a **syntax error** – in other words there is an error in the grammar of Visual Basic.

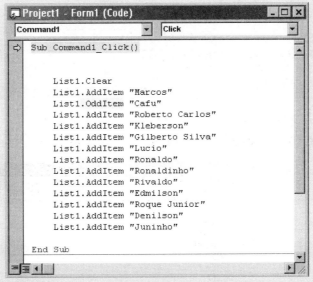

Figure 1.18 Visual Basic has found a syntax error in the fourth line of the instructions

3 Correct the error Visual Basic has found. Just double-click *OddItem* and retype it correctly as *AddItem*.

4 Test the program again by pressing F5 to re-run the program.

5 If Visual Basic finds any more errors it will react in the same way as before and you will have to correct further errors before the program can continue.

Save your project

As with most tasks you do at the computer, it is important to save your work. In Visual Basic, the first time you save a project two things are saved, the form and the project. Saving involves these steps:

1 From the **File** menu choose **Save Project**. The **Save File As** dialogue appears, as in Figure 1.19. Visual Basic prompts you for a name for your form and then for the project. You can use the same name for the form and the project.

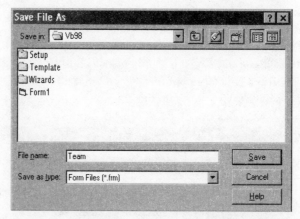

Figure 1.19
The Save File As
dialogue box

2 Type a name for Form1. For example, for the project above you could call it **Team**.

3 Click the **Save** button. The **Save Project As** dialogue appears, as in Figure 1.20.

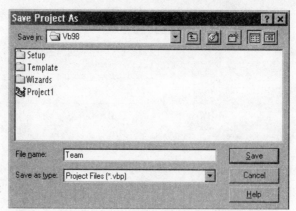

Figure 1.20
The Save Project
dialogue box

4 Give your Project1 a name. You can use the same name as the form.

If you make further changes to the project, Visual Basic will prompt you to save the changes before you close.

1.3 Displaying two lists

Adding a second list to a form

You can have more than one list on a form. This is just as well because you may want to give a bit more information about names appearing on your first list. How do you add another list?

The process is the same as for adding the first **List1**. You have to decide where on the form to place the new list box. In this case we want the information to come after the names of the footballers in List1. We will also need to increase the size of **Form1** so that the two lists can fit side by side. **Command1** will again do for filling both lists with the information. Visual Basic will call the second list box **List2**.

Plan for the form

- *Create two list boxes.*
- *Create two command buttons.*

Take a look back at Chapter 1.1 to see how you created List1, and create List2 in the same way.

Increase the size of Form1

If you move your cursor to the edge of the form you will find that the cursor becomes a double-arrowed pointer, which is a signal to you that if you drag with the mouse you can adjust the size of the form. Try it. Here are the steps again:

1 Move the mouse to the edge of the form.

2 When the cursor changes to a two-headed arrow, drag to size the form.

The program plan

Figure 1.21 shows a screenshot of the form after the extra **List2** box has been added. Notice that we have tried to make the two list boxes the same size, and List2 is positioned after **List1**. The command buttons are the same as before. **Command1** will hold the instructions to fill both List1 and List2. **Command2** will again end the program.

Let's write this down as a plan on separate lines – not in Visual Basic but in simple English sentences. We can call it our 'program plan'.

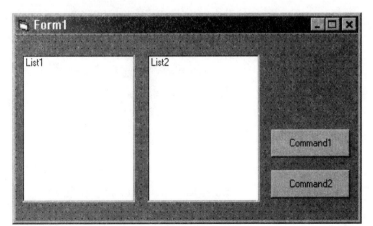

Figure 1.21 **List2** has been created on the form and sized to match **List1**

Plan for Command1 button

- Clear List1 with **List1.Clear**.
- Fill List1 with a list of names using **List1.AddItem** "…".
- Clear List2 with **List2.Clear**.
- Fill List2 with a list of positions using **List2.AddItem** "…".

Plan for Command2 button

- End the program.

Instructions for the command buttons

The code for the **Command1** button will be as follows:

```
List1.Clear
List1.AddItem "Marcos"
List1.AddItem "Cafu"
List1.AddItem "Roberto Carlos"
List1.AddItem "Kleberson"
List1.AddItem "Gilberto Silva"
List1.AddItem "Lucio"
List1.AddItem "Ronaldo"
List1.AddItem "Rivaldo"
List1.AddItem "Ronaldinho"
List1.AddItem "Edmilson"
List1.AddItem "Roque Junior"
List1.AddItem "Juninho"
List1.AddItem "Denilson"

List2.Clear
List2.AddItem "Goalkeeper"
List2.AddItem "Wing back"
List2.AddItem "Wing back "
List2.AddItem "Midfielder"
List2.AddItem "Back"
List2.AddItem "Back"
List2.AddItem "Forward"
List2.AddItem "Forward"
List2.AddItem "Forward"
List2.AddItem "Midfielder/Back"
List2.AddItem "Back"
List2.AddItem "Forward"
List2.AddItem "Forward"
```

Double-click the **Command1** control to get a code window and type these 28 lines into the button's click event, as in Figure 1.22. (Hint: When you are in the code window you can use, as in a word processor, 'copy and paste' rather than type the same thing again and again.)

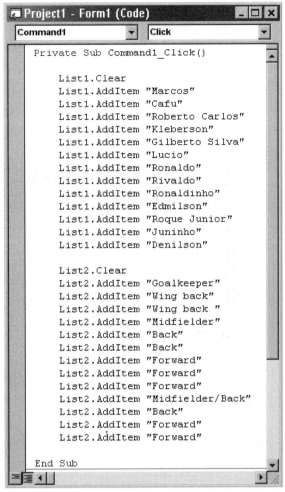

```
Project1 - Form1 (Code)
Command1                      Click

    Private Sub Command1_Click()

        List1.Clear
        List1.AddItem "Marcos"
        List1.AddItem "Cafu"
        List1.AddItem "Roberto Carlos"
        List1.AddItem "Kleberson"
        List1.AddItem "Gilberto Silva"
        List1.AddItem "Lucio"
        List1.AddItem "Ronaldo"
        List1.AddItem "Rivaldo"
        List1.AddItem "Ronaldinho"
        List1.AddItem "Edmilson"
        List1.AddItem "Roque Junior"
        List1.AddItem "Juninho"
        List1.AddItem "Denilson"

        List2.Clear
        List2.AddItem "Goalkeeper"
        List2.AddItem "Wing back"
        List2.AddItem "Wing back "
        List2.AddItem "Midfielder"
        List2.AddItem "Back"
        List2.AddItem "Back"
        List2.AddItem "Forward"
        List2.AddItem "Forward"
        List2.AddItem "Forward"
        List2.AddItem "Midfielder/Back"
        List2.AddItem "Back"
        List2.AddItem "Forward"
        List2.AddItem "Forward"

    End Sub
```

Figure 1.22 The code for **Command1** typed into the code window

The code for the **Command2** button will be:

End

This is shown in Figure 1.23.

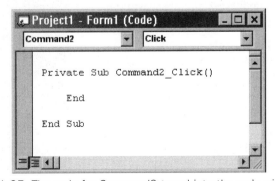

```
Project1 - Form1 (Code)
Command2                      Click

    Private Sub Command2_Click()

        End

    End Sub
```

Figure 1.23 The code for Command2 typed into the code window

Running the program

Press **F5** to run the program and click **Command1**. This time the two lists are filled with information. List1 again has the names of the players. List2 displays the positions of the players. When you clicked Command1, Visual Basic carried out the instructions that you typed into the button.

If your program stops with an error message, select **End** from the **Run** menu and refer back to the Help box on page 13.

Figure 1.24 shows what you will see if everything works out. Also test the **Command2** button to check that it ends your program.

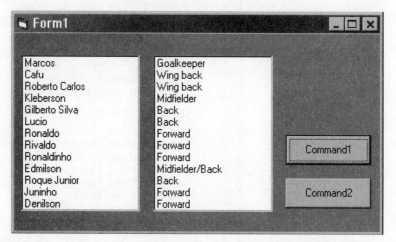

Figure 1.24 Both list boxes should be full when the **Command1** button is clicked

Save your project. I will call mine **Team Positions** this time.

 ### Now you try

Plan and write program instructions for these projects:

1 Display a list of names of ten of your school friends in one list box and their favourite pop groups in a second list box.

2 Display a list of names of six music groups and display them on the form. A second button should clear the list and display six songs. Use **List1.Clear** to clear the list box.

3 Use two list boxes to display a list of names of your favourite TV programmes in the first list box, and viewing times in the second list box only when a second button is clicked.

1.4 Listing in alphabetical order

Setting a property using the Properties Window

Any **object** that you create on a form has a set of **properties**. Properties can be used in Visual Basic to change how an object looks and behaves. In the following exercise you will learn how to use a property of a list box to make it display a list of names in alphabetical order.

Could we try to get the computer to put our previous list of names into alphabetical order? Is there a property of the list box that can do this for us? Let's try.

Use the project with the single list box that you saved in Chapter 1.2. When the form is open:

1 Click the **List1** box to select it.

2 Press **F4** to get the Property Window.

3 Set the **Sorted** property to **True** as shown in Figure 1.25.

4 Press **F5** to run your project and click on **Command1**.

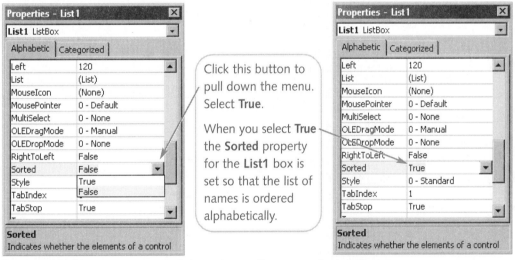

Click this button to pull down the menu. Select **True**.

When you select **True** the **Sorted** property for the **List1** box is set so that the list of names is ordered alphabetically.

Figure 1.25 Click the arrow to pull down the small menu, and select **True**

Make sure that you carry out the instructions and run the program to see whether the list is sorted. Your form should display the names sorted alphabetically, as in Figure 1.26.

Familiarise yourself with the method you have used to change the **Sorted** property for the list box. It will be used again to set other properties for objects in later projects.

Figure 1.26 Does your form now look like this?

Using the apostrophe (') and Rem

You can use the apostrophe symbol (') to write comments in your program. Anything after the ' symbol does not get done when the program is run, until a new line of programming starts without the apostrophe. You can also use **Rem** instead of the apostrophe. **Rem** is short for *Remark*. When you list your program instructions on the screen or the printer, the comments can be seen.

In the following example lines under **Command1_Click()** are comment lines and are ignored by Visual Basic when you run your program. They also may appear in a different colour:

```
Sub Command1_Click()

    'Program to sort a list of names by A. Pupil 1st February 1999
    'This program fills a list box with names of footballers

    List1.Clear
    List1.AddItem "Marcos"
    List1.AddItem "Cafu"
    List1.AddItem "Roberto Carlos"
    List1.AddItem "Kleberson"
    List1.AddItem "Gilberto Silva"
    List1.AddItem "Lucio"
    List1.AddItem "Ronaldo"
    List1.AddItem "Rivaldo"
    List1.AddItem "Ronaldinho"
    List1.AddItem "Edmilson"
    List1.AddItem "Roque Junior"
    List1.AddItem "Juninho"
    List1.AddItem "Denilson"

End Sub
```

Press **F5** to run your program, which will fill **List1** with the names of the footballers. The comments at the start of the program will have no effect on what the program does as they are ignored by Visual Basic. Try using the **Rem** keyword to make the same comments at the start of this program.

Save the changes to your project after you have added the comments to your program.

Why bother with comment lines?

Comment lines are used in programming to document things about the program you think are important. For example, a date can be inserted to show when the program was written. Someone reading your code listing might want to know who wrote the program, when it was written, and perhaps what the program is supposed to do. When programs become more complex and longer, comments can be used to explain what different parts of the program are supposed to do. This may also help if changes have to be made to the program.

Messages and program instructions and output with MsgBox

What is MsgBox?

In this chapter you will learn to use **MsgBox** (short for *Message Box*) to let you get information out of your program for the user to read. **MsgBox** is a Visual Basic function that can allow the programmer (that's you!) to display a message, an instruction or a result from the program. The user has to read the message and click **OK** before the program will continue.

Two examples

Look at Figure 1.27. What did the programmer have to do to get this message displayed on the screen?

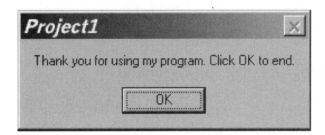

Figure 1.27 An example of a simple message using **MsgBox**

The **MsgBox** function needs to be told what the message is going to be, and the message *needs to be in quotes*. In this case the Visual Basic instruction was:

MsgBox "Thank you for using my program. Click OK to end."

That's all you, the programmer, have to do. Visual Basic takes care of the rest – such as placing the message on the screen, making the box the right size, and supplying the **OK** button for the user to press. So it does not matter how big your message is – all you have to make sure about is that it is within quotes.

Figure 1.28 shows another example. The Visual Basic instruction in this case was:

MsgBox "This program will allow you to enter 10 names and will sort them for you and display them in a list box. A. Pupil Feb. 2000"

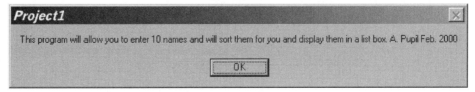

Figure 1.28 Another example of the use of **MsgBox**

You will find that **MsgBox** is a useful function to have as it allows you to interact with the user while the program is running. For example you can tell the user what to do next, explain what's going on, or give the result of a calculation.

In this chapter you will use **MsgBox** to display three messages – one message when the user clicks the **Command1** button and two more messages when the **Command2** button is clicked.

Let's start planning the program for this.

Program planning

The program will display three messages. The first message we want to appear as soon as the user clicks the **Command1** button, so the first **MsgBox** instruction will need to be right at the start, even before Visual Basic puts the names into **List1**. The message will tell the user what the program will do.

The next two messages we want to appear at the end, just before the program ends when the user clicks the **Command2** button. These two messages will say what has happened and thank the user for using the program.

We need a clear plan to detail exactly how this will be done.

Program plan for Command1

1 Display a message box.

2 Clear **List1**.

3 Add 13 names to **List1**.

The code for the **Command1** button will therefore be:

```
MsgBox "The program will sort a list of names"

List1.Clear
List1.AddItem "Marcos"
List1.AddItem "Cafu"
List1.AddItem "Roberto Carlos"
List1.AddItem "Kleberson"
List1.AddItem "Gilberto Silva"
List1.AddItem "Lucio"
List1.AddItem "Ronaldo"
List1.AddItem "Rivaldo"
List1.AddItem "Ronaldinho"
List1.AddItem "Edmilson"
List1.AddItem "Roque Junior"
List1.AddItem "Juninho"
List1.AddItem "Denilson"
```

Program plan for Command2

1 Display a message box.

2 Display another message box.

3 End the program.

The code for the **Command2** button will therefore be:

```
MsgBox "The program has sorted the list of names"
MsgBox "Thank you for using my program"
End
```

Writing the program

Opening your project

For this programming exercise you should open the very first program that you saved in Chapter 1.2. I called mine **Team**.

To open an existing project carry out these steps:

- From the **File** menu select **Open Project...**. The Open Project dialogue appears as in Figure 1.29. If you know where you saved the project, browse to it and click **Open**.

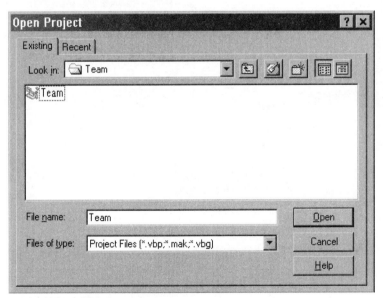

Figure 1.29 The Open Project dialogue box

- Alternatively, it is sometimes quicker to click the **Recent** tab, as in Figure 1.30 on the next page. You can do this because Visual Basic keeps track of the projects you have been creating recently to allow you to open the project you want with the **Recent** tab *shortcut*.

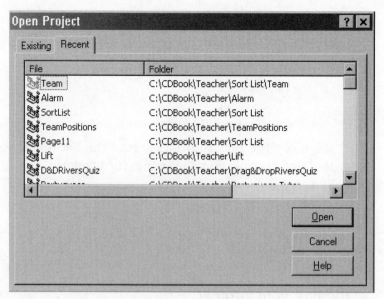

Figure 1.30 An alternative way to open a recent project, using the **Recent** tab shortcut

- Display the form for the project. If you do not see the form, select **Project Explorer** from the **View** menu. Then double-click the **Form** icon in **Project Explorer** (Figure 1.31). Form1 should now be visible, as in Figure 1.13 on page 9.

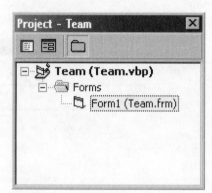

Figure 1.31 Opening a form project from within Project Explorer

Writing the code

1 Double-click the **Command1** button to open its code window.

2 Insert the **MsgBox** instruction for Command1 into the code window. The following extra line of code should go before **List1.Clear**:

```
MsgBox "The program will sort a list of names."
```

3 Now double-click the **Command2** button to open its code window. Insert the **MsgBox** instructions for Command2 into the code window, before **End**:

```
MsgBox "The program has sorted the list of names."
MsgBox "Thank you for using my program."
```

4 When you have typed the instructions into the buttons, press **F5** to run the program.

5 Now click the **Command1** button. The first message box appears, as in Figure 1.32. Click **OK** to continue. The form displays the list sorted, as in Figure 1.33.

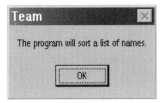

Figure 1.32
The first message box

Figure 1.33 The sorted list is displayed

6 Now click the **Command2** button. The second message box appears, as in Figure 1.34. Click **OK** to continue and the third message box appears.

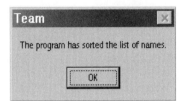 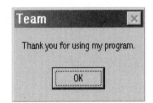

Figure 1.34 The second and third message boxes

7 Click **OK** again and the program ends.

Save your project

Save your project once you have successfully tested it. If your program stops with an error message, select **End** from the **Run** menu.

If you are told of an error when you run the program you will need to fix the error and try running the program again. Refer to the Help section on page 13 for information on fixing errors.

 Now you try

Amend the program that you named 'Team Positions' so that the list boxes display in alphabetical order.

Be careful with any projects that use two list boxes. After alphabetical sorting the second list box will no longer correspond to the names in the first box! For the moment just use one list box, e.g.:

    List1.AddItem "A. Teacher, ... A Subject"

like this:

    List1.AddItem "Mr Einstein, ... Physics"

A task that you will be asked to do is to produce a printout of the instructions in your program. This is called a **code listing**. It contains all the instructions including the comments that you typed into any of the buttons while you were designing and creating the program.

The printout can be used as evidence that you did indeed produce the instructions that allowed your program to run successfully. You can also use the code listing to troubleshoot errors in your code, which can sometimes prove difficult on the screen.

Follow the instructions below to produce a printout of the coding for the project you have just completed.

Printing your code

1 Select **Print**... from the **File** menu. The dialogue box in Figure 1.35 appears.

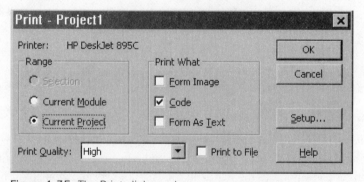

Figure 1.35 The Print dialogue box

2 The **Current Project** option button should be selected.

3 The **Code** check-box should be checked and the other two *not*. Now click **OK**.

Making a screen dump of your program running

If you need to show evidence of your program output, then this is a way to do it:

1 First make sure that the form you want to dump to the printer is the active window. If it is not, click on it or do **Alt + Tab** until it is.

2 Now do **Alt + PrintScreen**. This will copy the form into the Windows clipboard.

3 Run **MSPaint** or another program with graphics, and paste **(Ctrl + V)**.

4 Use the graphics program to print the image of your form and program output. If you use a Windows word processor like **Word** you can document, in addition, what's happening.

Ask your teacher or tutor to demonstrate this for you if you get into difficulties. The usual locations of **Tab**, **Alt** and **PrintScreen** are shown in Figure 1.36

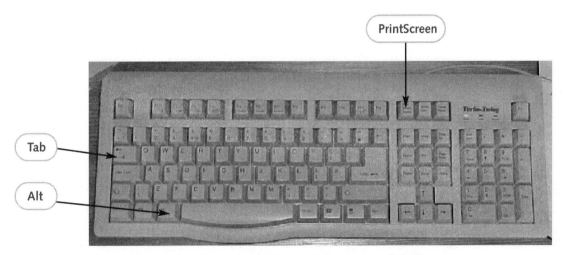

Figure 1.36 The usual keyboard positions of **Tab**, **Alt** and **PrintScreen**

1.8 InputBox

Getting data into the computer

Visual Basic lets us get **input** (data) into the computer by supplying us with a dialogue box that uses a function called **InputBox**. You use the *input box* to ask the user for information which you can then get the program to put into a *list box*. The user types data into the input box's *text area*.

You, the programmer, have to decide what the prompt to the user is going to be, so that the user knows what kind of information to type in.

You have also to decide a name for the **variable** that will hold the information the user types in.

Figure 1.37 shows an example of what an input box looks like to the user of a program. When presented with this the user will have to read the prompt that appears. In this case the prompt is 'Please enter a name.' The user then types a name into the text box input area – the user in this example has typed 'Peggy'.

As with MsgBox, you do not have to worry about where the input box will be placed, or its size. Visual Basic does all that. Visual Basic also supplies the two buttons for **OK** and **Cancel**.

Figure 1.37 The result of using the function **InputBox**

If the user now clicks **OK** (or presses **Enter** on the keyboard) anything typed into the text box will be stored in the computer's memory. Clicking **Cancel** will clear the input box and nothing will be stored in the computer's memory.

In this example, to get the input box displayed on the screen you will have used the instruction:

```
FriendsName = InputBox("Please enter a name.")
```

Each part of the instruction is important, so let's study it in detail.

Understanding InputBox

In its simplest form the **InputBox** instruction is made up of four parts (see Figure 1.38):

1 The **variable** to hold in the computer's memory whatever the user types in.

2 The = sign to set the variable to whatever the user enters.

3 The **InputBox** function itself.

4 The **prompt** for the user, in brackets and in double quotes.

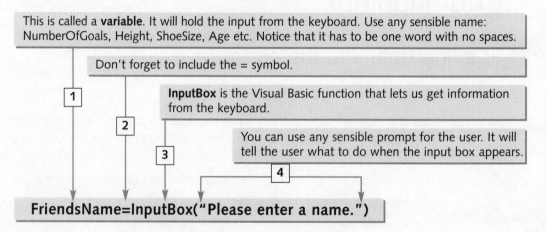

Figure 1.38 Elements of the **InputBox** instruction line

More about the variable FriendsName

In the example in Figure 1.37 the variable **FriendsName** would hold the data 'Peggy' when the user clicks **OK**. If the user instead clicked **Cancel** the input box would close and nothing would be stored in the computer's memory.

If the user did indeed enter 'Peggy' then you would be able to use the variable **FriendsName** later in the program. For example you could subsequently use the instruction:

```
List1.AddItem FriendsName
```

Visual Basic would display whatever the user happened to enter – in this case, 'Peggy'.

The two instructions in the **Command1** button:

```
FriendsName = InputBox("Please enter a name.")
List1.AddItem FriendsName
```

would produce an output from the program as shown in Figure 1.39.

Figure 1.39 What happens when the user clicks on **OK**

Jargon buster

String – The variable **FriendsName** is an example of a string variable. A string is a word or phrase made up of keyboard characters. For example, in Visual Basic you could create a string variable with a statement like this:

```
UserHobby = "Cycling"
```

In this example the variable is **UserHobby** and it has been set to hold the string "Cycling". The quotes around the string tells Visual Basic that we want the variable **UserHobby** to be treated as a string variable.

In a program using **InputBox** we could also set the **UserHobby** variable. For example:

```
UserHobby = InputBox("What is your hobby?")
```

Whatever input the user types in would be treated as a string and would be held in the **UserHobby** variable.

Planning the form

In this project you will learn to use **InputBox** to call up your friends' names along with their phone numbers. Again you will use a list box. We need to design the form and its objects and the instructions for our program to get the details in.

We are going to use a new object called a **label**. Labels allow us to place headings and instructions on a form.

On the form, the heading 'My Party List' is a label with its **Caption** property set to **My Party List** and its **Font** property set to bold and size larger than 12pt. You will be shown next how to create the label and how to change the properties of the objects so that the form displays as you see in Figure 1.40.

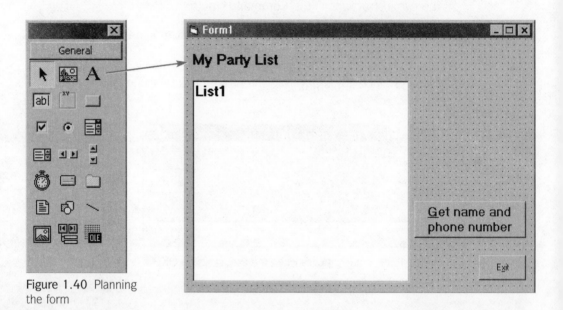

Figure 1.40 Planning the form

Jargon buster

Variable – A variable is a single memory element that is given a name and that during the runtime life of a program can be set to a value whenever the programmer requires it. The variable can have its value changed at various times depending on how it is used in the program.

The programmer will normally invent a suitably meaningful name for the variable depending on what it is going to be used for. For example, if the variable is going to hold the names of friends, a suitable name would be **FriendsName**. Choosing meaningful names for variables will make the program code more readable.

Naming of variables – A variable name can be up to 255 characters long, made up of letters, numbers and the underscore character.

- The name must start with a letter.
- There must be no spaces or other symbols in the name.
- Upper and lower case letters are treated as being the same.
- You must not use **reserved** words (names that Visual Basic uses for special purposes, like **If** or **Loop**).

Plan for the form

First create a label:

1 Use the Toolbox to create a **Label1** on the form. The label control on the Toolbox is the capital A.

2 Drag out the shape for the label so that it is about 75mm wide and 12mm in height.

3 Select the label you have just created and press **F4**. The properties for the label should be visible, as in Figure 1.41.

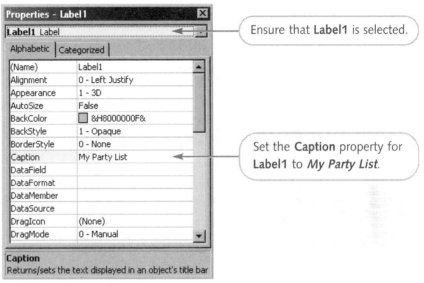

Figure 1.41 The **Properties** dialogue box

4 Set the **Caption** property for **Label1** to My Party List.

5 With the label still selected, go to its **Font** property and click on the ellipsis button to reveal the **Font dialogue**, as in Figure 1.42. The **Font dialogue** appears as in Figure 1.43.

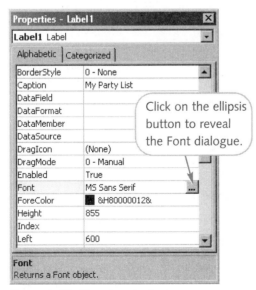

Figure 1.42 Choosing the font

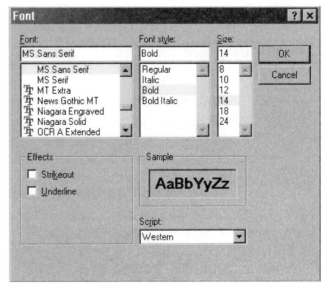

Figure 1.43 The **Font** dialogue box

6 Select a font and set the style to bold and the size to 14pt. Click **OK**.

7 Place the label you have designed in the top left of the form.

Next create a list box on Form1 by using the **ListBox** control. Visual Basic calls it **List1**. Set its **Font** property to 14pt.

You now need to create two command buttons using the **Button** control. The method to change the caption and font properties of a button is the same as you learned for the label earlier in the chapter.

- The caption property for the first button should be **Get name and phone number** and its font property set to 14pt.

- The caption property for the second button should be **Exit** and its font property set to 10pt.

The form when you have finished designing it should look like the one in Figure 1.44. You have finished planning the form so it is now time to plan the program.

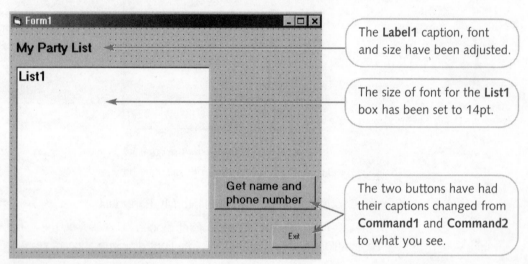

Figure 1.44 The final form plan

Writing the program

Plan for button *Get name and phone number*

1 Get the name using **InputBox**.
2 Get the phone number using **InputBox**.
3 Add the name and number to **List1** with **AddItem**.

Code for button *Get name and phone number*

Double-click the button **Get name and phone number** and type the three lines you see in Figure 1.45 into its click event.

Plan for button *Exit*

This button will end the program.

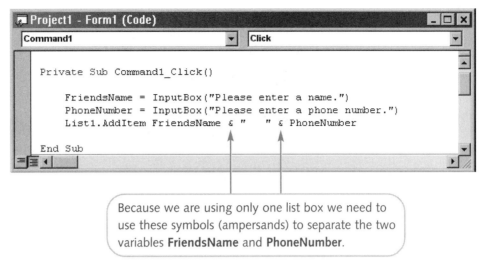

Because we are using only one list box we need to use these symbols (ampersands) to separate the two variables **FriendsName** and **PhoneNumber**.

Figure 1.45 The code for the first button

Code for button *Exit*

Double-click the button **Exit** to get its code window and type **End** into its click event, as in Figure 1.46.

Figure 1.46 The code for the **Exit** button to end the program

Press F5 to run and test your project.

Running and testing the program

Click the button **Get name and phone number** for each name that you want to enter into the program. The program will prompt first for the name and then for the phone number, as in Figure 1.47.

The names and numbers will be inserted into the list box as the **InputBoxes** are processed. You should end up with a form similar to the one in Figure 1.48 on the next page.

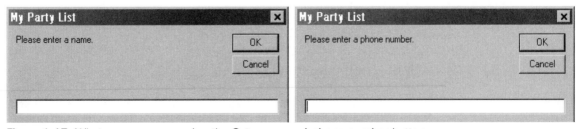

Figure 1.47 What you see on pressing the **Get name and phone number** button

Figure 1.48 The list box starts to take shape

Don't forget to save your project.

An important note on planning your projects

In every problem that you tackle it is a very good idea to follow a certain sequence of actions, to ensure that nothing is forgotten. The following is a suggested list of actions to help you.

1 Sketch neatly on paper the design for any form(s) that your project contains, with controls such as labels and buttons clearly marked.

2 Write a plan of the steps that your program will have to take. Use short English sentences and a separate line for each action.

3 Only now write the actual Visual Basic coding for any program instructions that your program will have to carry out.

4 When your program is working properly, print out a listing of the program code, as you have been shown.

5 Take screen shots of your program running, as you have learned, and print them as evidence that your program works.

6 Make sure your name is on all printed output and give it to your teacher or tutor.

7 Discuss with your teacher or tutor any difficulties you had with the project and suggest improvements.

Now you try

Use **InputBox** to get the information for the list boxes you use. Remember to use the method: **List1.AddItem** *Variable*. The variable holds whatever the user enters into **InputBox**.

You have already created projects that you can modify to carry out the following tasks.

1 Draw up a list of names of ten of your friends and their favourite music groups. Display the information in a list box. Create a button that the user can click to clear the list box.

2 Display a list of names of six sports groups and display them on the form. Sort the list box alphabetically.

Remember that you must, for each program that you write, have a:

- program plan – a step-by-step plan in your own words
- a form design showing the objects on your human–computer interface (HCI)
- a code listing (see Chapter 1.7 for help on printing).

1.9 More on list boxes

You have learned how to create and use a list box. You made use of the **AddItem** method to *add* items to a list box.

Visual Basic lets you do more with a list box than just add items to it. You can also ask Visual Basic to *remove* an item from the list. This is definitely a useful feature for your program because the user might make a mistake and want to remove an entry or change an entry.

You will now learn to use the **RemoveItem** method with a list box to remove the *last* item that was entered, and then to remove *any* item that the user highlights.

Removing the last item entered

Planning the form

You will be able to use the project that you created for the last chapter. You will be adding another button to the form. The form of your last project should look something like Figure 1.49 on the next page.

We need to create another button on the form that will allow the user to click it and *remove the last item only* from the list. We therefore need to change the form's design so that it looks like Figure 1.50.

Create the new button you see in the figure and change its caption property to **Remove last item only**. Set its font property to 12pt.

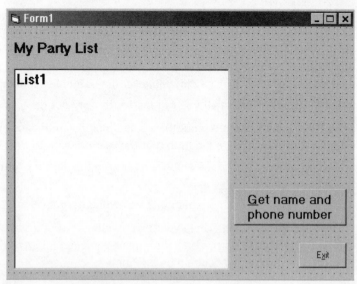

Figure 1.49 The starting point for this project

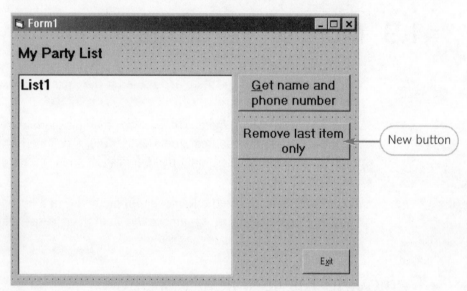

Figure 1.50 The new plan for the form

Writing the program

All we have to do is add one line of instruction to the new button. The new piece of code will remove the last item in the list.

Code for button *Remove last item only*

The additional code line is:

```
List1.RemoveItem List1.ListCount -1
```

Double-click the button to bring up its code window and type the line into its click event, as in Figure 1.51.

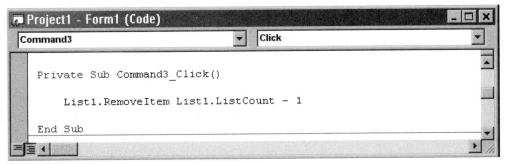

Figure 1.51 The code window with the line of code typed in

Testing the program

Run and test your updated program. Use the **Get name and phone number** button first to produce a list in the list box. Once you have several items in the list, click the **Remove last item only** button to remove the last item.

If you receive an error message like the one in Figure 1.52, it probably means that there are no items in the list. If this happens, just click the **End** button and run the program again and make sure you enter some names and numbers into the list box.

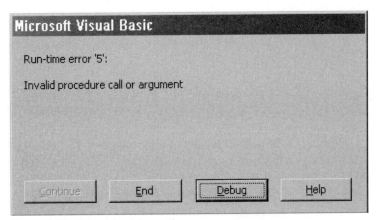

Figure 1.52 Visual Basic's runtime error message

When your program is successfully removing the last item in the list, save the program.

Jargon buster

ListCount – The ListCount property gives you the number of the items in a filled list. Lists in Visual Basic are numbered from 0, so a list with six items would be numbered 0, 1, 2, 3, 4 and 5. To refer to the *last item*, therefore, the Visual Basic statement would be **List1Count -1**.

Removing any item from the list

Planning the form

Again, you will be able to use the same project as above. You will be adding another button to the form that will allow the user to click it and **remove a highlighted item** from the list. We need to change the form's design so that it looks like Figure 1.53.

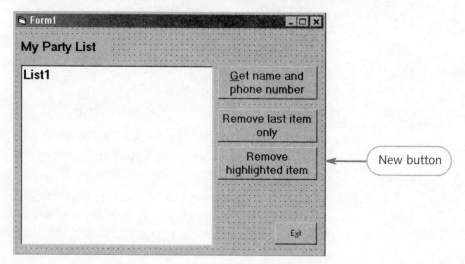

Figure 1.53 The new plan for an additional button

Create the new button you see and change its caption property to **Remove highlighted item**. Set its font property to 12pt.

Writing the program

Again we simply have to add one more line of instruction for the new button. The new piece of code will remove the highlighted item in the list.

Code for button *Remove highlighted item*

The additional code line is:

```
List1.RemoveItem List1.ListIndex
```

Double-click the button to bring up its code window and type the line into its click event, as in Figure 1.54.

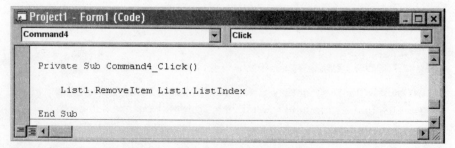

Figure 1.54 The code window with the line of code typed in

Testing the program

Run and test your updated program. Use the **Get name and phone number** button first so that you get a list into the list box. Once you have several items in the list click the **Remove highlighted item** button to remove the highlighted item.

If you receive an error message like the one shown earlier in Figure 1.52, again it probably means that there are no items in the list. If this happens, click the **End** button and run the program again and make sure you enter some names and numbers into the list box.

When your program is successfully removing the highlighted item in the list, save the program.

Jargon buster

ListIndex – The ListIndex property gives you the number of the item that is currently highlighted in a list box.

Now you try

Supertask

Use the skills you have learned in this chapter to improve on the last project you created. Create a new project that has *two list boxes*. Use one of the list boxes to display your friends' names and the second list box to display the phone numbers for those friends. Offer the user four buttons on the form:

1 one button to get the names and phone numbers in the two *separate* lists

2 one button to delete the last item in *both* lists

3 one button to clear *both* list boxes of all the items

4 an Exit button to stop the program.

Use **InputBox** to get the information for the list boxes you use. Remember to use the method: **List1.AddItem** *Variable.* The variable holds whatever the user enters into the input box.

Use **List1.RemoveItem List1.ListCount -1** to remove the last item in a list.

Designing the human–computer interface (HCI)

We have spent quite a bit of time and effort in making sure that what the user sees of our programs is clear and what they are expected to do is easy to understand. We try to achieve this by placing, on the form, **label** objects and by having meaningful captions on command buttons. The form we use in a project is our **human–computer interface**, which is usually abbreviated to HCI. The form and its objects allow the user to communicate with the computer.

The human–computer interface is any program or piece of hardware that allows the user to communicate with the computer. In this book the term 'HCI' will be used mainly to mean the form and the objects on the form. So when we design the HCI we are creating the form that will let the user interact with the computer via our program.

In completing the project in this chapter you will learn how to use **text boxes** to get input from the user and how to do calculations with that input.

A program to perform addition

We shall be creating a project to act as a simple **adding** program to enable a user to add two numbers together. We will need to create **text boxes** where the user can type in the numbers to be added, and a **label** object to display the result. We will need a plus sign and an equals sign, which will come from the Visual Basics Toolbox. We will also need a command button programmed to calculate the result, and a button to exit the program.

Computers are great at arithmetic. When they add, subtract, multiply and divide, the signs they use are in some cases different from the ones you use in maths. The keyboard signs used are:

+ means 'add'	– means 'subtract'
* means 'multiply'	/ means 'divide'

Here are some examples:

You want to:	On the computer do:
Add 8 and 2	Answer = 8 + 2
Subtract 2 from 8	Answer = 8 – 2
Multiply 8 by 2	Answer = 8 * 2
Divide 8 by 2	Answer = 8 / 2

'Answer' in the table above is an example of a numerical **variable** because it can hold various number values at different times in the running of a program. Once it has a value you can display it in an object on a form. For example:

```
List1.AddItem answer
```

or

```
Label1.Caption = answer
```

If you want to use data that a user types into a text box to do arithmetic with it, you need to use the function **Val** (short for value). It makes Visual Basic treat what is in a text box as a numeric value. For example:

```
Answer = Val(Text1) + Val(Text2)
```

We will see how to do this in our project for the **adding** program. The next chapter will look at a calculator program.

Jargon buster

The variable **Answer** used in the text is an example of a numerical variable. A numerical variable can contain a number. For example, in Visual Basic you could create a numerical variable with a statement like this:

```
MyAge = 15
```

In this example the variable is **MyAge** and it has been set to hold the value 15. Because there are no quotes around the number 15, Visual Basic determines that we want the variable **MyAge** to *be treated as a numerical variable*.

In a program using **InputBox** we could also set the **Answer** variable. For example:

```
MyAge = InputBox("What is your age?")
```

Whatever number input the user types in would be treated as a number and would be held in the **MyAge** variable. We could then display it in a label or list box. For example:

```
Label1.Caption = MyAge
List1.AddItem MyAge
```

Planning the form for the Adding program

Now we will design the human–computer interface for the adding program. In this project we are going to use two text boxes. A text box allows the user to input data into the program when it is running. A label does not allow input from the keyboard at runtime.

Plan for the form

We wish to:

1 create two **text boxes**
2 create three **labels**
3 create two **command buttons**
4 create two **arithmetic symbols** using the **line** control.

You have not met a text box before. Use the **TextBox** control in the Toolbox shown in Figure 1.55. Use the same skills you learned for creating labels and command buttons.

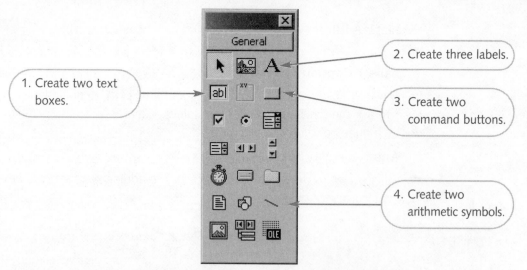

1. Create two text boxes.

2. Create three labels.

3. Create two command buttons.

4. Create two arithmetic symbols.

Figure 1.55 What you will need from the Visual Basic Toolbox

To draw the arithmetic symbols '+' and '=', click on the line tool ('\').

Make sure that you place the text boxes and labels *exactly* as you see in the top part of Figure 1.56 or your program's results will not be displayed correctly.

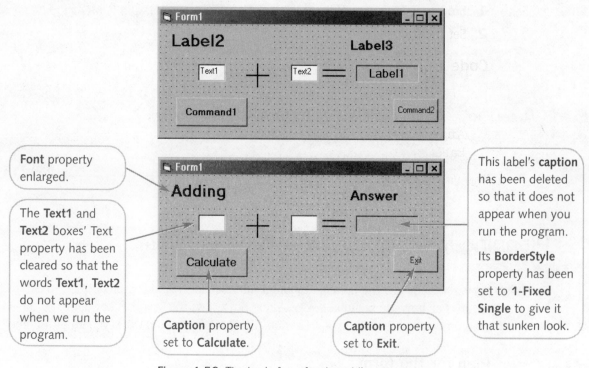

Font property enlarged.

The **Text1** and **Text2** boxes' Text property has been cleared so that the words **Text1**, **Text2** do not appear when we run the program.

Caption property set to **Calculate**.

Caption property set to **Exit**.

This label's **caption** has been deleted so that it does not appear when you run the program.

Its **BorderStyle** property has been set to **1-Fixed Single** to give it that sunken look.

Figure 1.56 The basic form for the adding program

Improving the HCI

Change the *properties* of the objects to achieve what you see in the lower part of Figure 1.56. Use the **Properties** window as you learnt in earlier chapters. For example, change the captions on labels. Alter the font properties for the command buttons, text boxes and labels.

Making the changes to the HCI

1 Set the caption property for Label2 to **Adding** and the font to bold 14pt.

2 Set the caption property for Label3 to **Answer** and the font to bold 12pt.

3 Set the **BorderStyle** property for Label1 to **1 – Fixed Single** to give the label the sunken look. Also delete its caption altogether.

4 Delete the **Text** property for both Text1 and Text2. Leave the properties blank. This will mean that when the program is run the text boxes will be blank ready to accept user input.

5 Change the captions for the buttons to **Calculate** and **Exit**.

6 Change the **BorderWidth** property of the arithmetic symbols to **2** to make them bolder.

Writing the program

You are going to create a program to add two numbers together. The user will enter two numbers into the text boxes and when the **Calculate** button is clicked Visual Basic will add them together and place the answer into the sunken Label1.

Plan for the *Calculate* button

1 Set the variable **Answer** to the value of **Text1** plus the value of **Text2**.

2 Set **Label1**'s caption to **Answer**.

Code for the *Calculate* button

Double-click the button to bring up its code window and type the instruction into it, as in Figure 1.57. The required code is:

```
Answer = Val(Text1) + Val(Text2)
Label1.Caption = Answer
```

This Visual Basic instruction tells the program to set the caption of Label1 to the value that is in Text1 and also add the value that is in Text2 to it. Label1 will then show the result of the addition (answer).

Plan for the *Exit* button

Clicking on the Exit button should stop the program running.

Code for the *Exit* button

Double-click the button to bring up its code window and type the instruction into it, as in Figure 1.57. The required code is: **End**

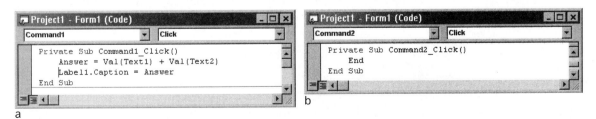

Figure 1.57 The code windows for the **Calculate** and **Exit** buttons

Running and testing the program

Test your project by pressing **F5** to run the program and type numbers into the text boxes. Click the **Calculate** button to see the result. Make sure the program is producing the correct results.

If your program stops with an error, *Visual Basic will highlight the line that is causing the problem*. Correct it and press F5 again.

If everything has gone according to plan, when the program has been run and numbers have been entered into the text boxes the form should resemble the example in Figure 1.58, with the correct results in the answer label on the right of the form.

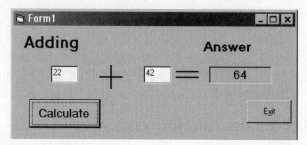

Figure 1.58 A typical result of running the adding program

If wrong results are presented by the program, make sure that you have placed the label and text boxes in the correct positions relative to each other. Also check that you have placed this command into the **Calculate** button:

```
Answer = Val(Text1) + Val(Text2)
Label1.Caption = Answer
```

It is very important that you type the commands exactly as you see them, or Visual Basic will not understand what is to be done and will produce an error. Your program stops with an error select **End** from the **Run** menu.

Remember to save your project when it is producing the correct results.

 Now you try

Re-open the **Adding** project you created to help you to carry out the following task.

Create a new project to calculate the area of a rectangle when the user supplies the length and breadth. As you will *not* be adding the values to find the area, you will have to make a simple change to the program instructions so that a correct calculation is carried out – multiplication.

Make your form's HCI easy for the user to understand, where the length and breadth are to be typed into text boxes. Since *area* is *length* multiplied by *breadth*, you will need to change the HCI to show that you will multiply the two values entered by the user.

Remember that you must, for each program that you write, have:

- a program plan – a step-by-step plan in your own words
- a form design showing the objects on your human-computer interface (HCI)
- a code listing (see Chapter 1.7 for help on printing).

A calculator program

If you managed to create the simple adding program in the last chapter it will be an easy step to create a basic calculator. With this the user will be able to add, subtract, multiply and divide. As before we will need to create **text boxes** where the user can type in numbers, **label** objects to display results, and **arithmetic symbols** with the Visual Basic Toolbox. We will also need **command buttons** programmed to calculate results and to exit the program. You may wish to look back at the last chapter to remind yourself of the symbols computers use to do arithmetic.

Planning the human–computer interface

This is the plan:

1 create seven **labels**

2 create two **command buttons**

3 create eight **text boxes**.

As before, make sure that you place the text boxes and labels exactly as you see in Figure 1.59, otherwise your program's results will not be displayed correctly.

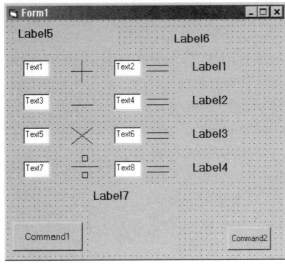

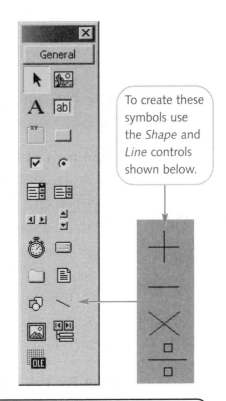

To create these symbols use the *Shape* and *Line* controls shown below.

Figure 1.59 Plan for the calculator form

Hint: To align objects quickly, either horizontally or vertically, highlight the objects as a block by holding the Shift key down and clicking on each control to be aligned. Then go to the **Format** menu and choose **Align**.

Improving the HCI

Change the properties of the objects to achieve what you see on the form in Figure 1.60. For example, delete the captions on labels 1 to 4, and alter the font properties for the command buttons, text boxes and labels.

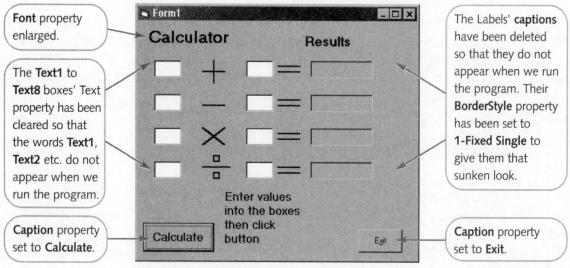

Font property enlarged.

The **Text1** to **Text8** boxes' Text property has been cleared so that the words **Text1**, **Text2** etc. do not appear when we run the program.

Caption property set to **Calculate**.

The Labels' **captions** have been deleted so that they do not appear when we run the program. Their **BorderStyle** property has been set to **1-Fixed Single** to give them that sunken look.

Caption property set to **Exit**.

Figure 1.60 The improved interface

Planning the program

Plan for the *Calculate* button (English language version)

1 Set the variable **AdditionAnswer** to the value of Text1 plus the value of Text2.

2 Set **Label1**'s caption to **AdditionAnswer**.

3 Set the variable **SubtractionAnswer** to the value of Text3 minus the value of Text4.

4 Set **Label2**'s caption to **SubtractionAnswer**.

5 Set the variable **MultiplicationAnswer** to the value of Text5 times the value of Text6.

6 Set **Label3**'s caption to **MultiplicationAnswer**.

7 Set the variable **DivisionAnswer** to the value of Text7 divided by the value of Text8.

8 Set **Label4**'s caption to **DivisionAnswer**.

Plan for the *Calculate* button (structure diagram version)

Some programmers when designing a computer program find it useful to draw a structure diagram to describe what the program is supposed to do. A structure diagram is a good way of seeing the overall picture of a program without having to read through all the lines of code. Figure 1.61 shows a structure diagram for this calculator program.

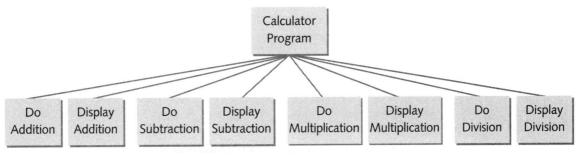

Figure 1.61 The structure of the calculator program

The box at the top tells you what the program will do. The boxes below are arranged from left to right *in the order in which the instructions in the program will be carried out*. Unit 4 and the document 'Using a structure diagram' on your CD-ROM have more information on how to use a structure diagram.

Code for the *Calculate* button

The required code is:

```
AdditionAnswer = Val(Text1) + Val(Text2)
Label1.Caption = AdditionAnswer
SubtractionAnswer = Val(Text3) – Val(Text4)
Label2.Caption = SubtractionAnswer
MultiplicationAnswer = Val(Text5) * Val(Text6)
Label3.Caption = MultiplicationAnswer
DivisionAnswer = Val(Text7) / Val(Text8)
Label4.Caption = DivisionAnswer
```

Double-click the button to bring up its code window and type those instructions into it, as shown in Figure 1.62. The spaces between the lines are optional and do not affect the running of the program.

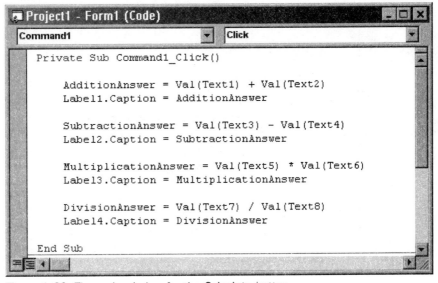

Figure 1.62 The code window for the **Calculate** button

Plan for the *Exit* button

Clicking on this button at runtime will stop the program running.

Code for the *Exit* button

Double-click the button to bring up its code window and type the instruction into it as shown in Figure 1.63.

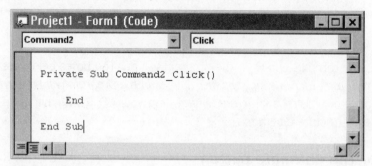

Figure 1.63 The code window for the **Exit** button

Avoiding an overflow error

Before you run your program we have to guard against an **overflow error**.

Computers do not like having to divide by zero, so we have to make sure that **Text8** is set to greater than zero when the program runs. Double-click the form to open up its **Form_Load** procedure, as in the top part of Figure 1.64. Type this line of code into the code window:

```
Text8 = 1
```

This bit of code will prevent this particular overflow error.

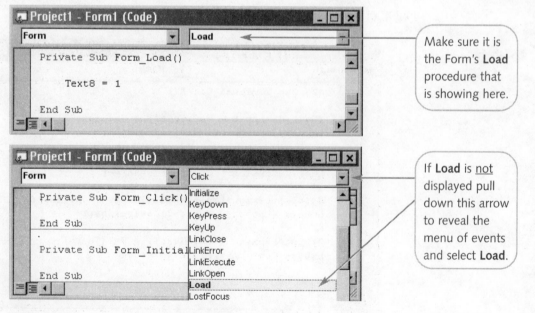

Figure 1.64 Getting the Form_Load procedure window

A note on the Val function

You really need to use 'Val' only when you are using the + operator, although your code often makes more sense to a reader with all the 'Val's left in. So the code above *could* also have been:

```
AdditionAnswer = Val(Text1) + Val(Text2)
Label1.Caption = AdditionAnswer
SubtractionAnswer = Text3 – Text4
Label2.Caption = SubtractionAnswer
MultiplicationAnswer = Text5 * Text6
Label3.Caption = MultiplicationAnswer
DivisionAnswer = Text7 / Text8
Label4.Caption = DivisionAnswer
```

Why does the + operator need **Val** and not the others? In Chapter 1.8 you read that a **string** is a sequence of characters. Visual Basic can combine strings to form other strings, like this:

```
MyFriend = "Helen"
MyFeelings = "I love"
Aspace = " "
Message = MyFeelings + Aspace + MyFriend
Label1.Caption = Message
```

The Label1 would display 'I love Helen'.

In our program, if the user entered a 2 into Text1 and a 2 into Text2 and you had not used **Val**, the answer in Label1 would show 22 and not 4 as expected. Visual Basic would treat *each* entry as a string because the default value for a text box is of the string type.

You will learn more about strings later.

Running and testing the program

Test your project by pressing **F5** to run the program and type numbers into the text boxes. Click the **Calculate** button to see the results on the right of the form. Make sure the program is producing the correct results. The example in Figure 1.65 shows how the calculator program should perform when it is run.

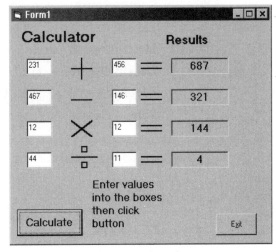

Figure 1.65 The calculator in action

Use a calculator, or the one supplied in the Windows Accessories programs group, to see that you get the right answers for a set of numbers. Here is a set for you to try:

Operation	First text box	Second text box	Answer
Adding	16	23	39
Subtracting	67	42	25
Multiplying	12	12	144
Dividing	88	11	8

Troubleshooting

If the program stops with an error, select **End** from the **Run** menu. *Visual Basic will highlight the line that is causing the problem.* Try to correct the error and press F5 again.

Labels and commands

If the program runs but the wrong results show up, make sure that you have placed the labels in the correct positions.

If the labels are in the correct positions and one or more of the answers is still wrong then you may have introduced a **logic error** into the coding. The program does not stop running but it does not give the correct answers. The Help box opposite goes into detail about logic arrors.

Also check that you have placed these commands into the **Calculate** button:

```
AdditionAnswer = Val(Text1) + Val(Text2)
Label1.Caption = AdditionAnswer
SubtractionAnswer = Val(Text3) – Val(Text4)
Label2.Caption = SubtractionAnswer
MultiplicationAnswer = Val(Text5) * Val(Text6)
Label3.Caption = MultiplicationAnswer
DivisionAnswer = Val(Text7) / Val(Text8)
Label4.Caption = DivisionAnswer
```

It is important that you type these commands exactly or Visual Basic will not understand what it has to do and will come up with an error.

Help

Logic errors

If your program gives incorrect results for calculations, it *might* mean that you have introduced a logic error into the program. Let's see how this can happen.

For example, take multiplication. You have entered 12 into the first text box and 12 into the second text box and expect 144 to appear in the label to the right, but the label displays a 1 instead. The program has not stopped running, but neither is it working properly because it has given the wrong answer. A logic error might be the cause.

On looking closely at the coding you notice that something is wrong:

```
MultiplicationAnswer = Val(Text5) / Val(Text6)

Label3.Caption = MultiplicationAnswer
```

Clearly you have used the wrong symbol in the instruction: a '/' for division instead of a '*' for multiplication. *That is a logic error.*

So you correct the logic error by replacing the incorrect symbol, and on running the program again you are glad to see that the multiplication calculations are OK.

Unfortunately, logic errors are not always as easy to correct as that. In fact, logic errors can be a great nuisance because they can lull you into a false sense of security. You might think 'My program does not crash and seems to work all right', even though a logic error may be present but does not show itself with simple testing.

It is therefore important to test your programs with data for which you know the correct answers for calculations done on those data. *Always test your programs with care.*

Jargon buster

Bugs and debugging – A bug is an error in the structure or detail of a program that causes the program to go wrong (*malfunction*) in some way. The term came about in the early days of computing, when real insects (bugs) would get caught in the internal wiring of computer logic circuits, causing the computer to malfunction and the programs to crash. Computer technicians would have to physically 'debug' the hardware by removing the winged or legged insects from inside the computer cabinet.

So far you have met two types of bugs or errors – **syntax** errors in Chapter 2 and **logic** errors in this chapter.

What's the difference between a syntax error and a logic error? Can you guess? A syntax error will stop the program running and you have to correct the error before you can continue. A logic error, in contrast, can go unnoticed because the program will seem to run all right but it will give incorrect results. Imagine you programmed a navigation system for a rocket to go to Mars and it arrived at Venus! The navigation system did not cause the rocket to crash, but the destination was wrong – a logic error!

Now you try

Improve the calculator project you have just completed by giving the user the choice of what type of calculation is required. This can be achieved by having four buttons rather than the single **Calculate** button. The user clicks on one of four buttons: Add, Subtract, Multiply or Divide.

Two numbers should be the input via two text boxes and the answer displayed in a label. Figure 1.66 shows what you should try to achieve. Think what should happen when a user clicks on any of the buttons. This design represents a user-friendlier HCI with fewer objects on the form.

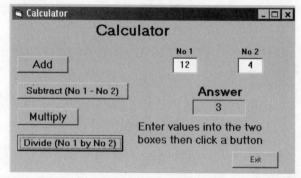

Figure 1.66 The design for an improved calculator project

Now you try

Supertask

Use the ideas from the **Calculator** program you created to help you to carry out the following task. You will need to start a new project.

Design the HCI shown in Figure 1.67 to allow conversion from pounds sterling to common world currencies. Here is a hint for coding the Dollars button:

The *name* property for this text box should be **txtPounds**

The *name* property for these buttons should be:

cmdEuros
cmdDollars
cmdRupees
cmdRand
cmdUpToYou!

The *name* property for these labels should be:

lblEuros
lblDollars
lblRupees
lblRand
lblUpToYou!

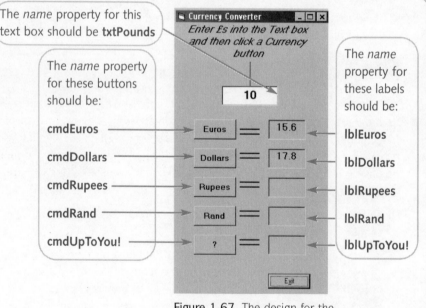

Figure 1.67 The design for the currency converter

```
Private Sub cmdDollars_Click()
    NumberOfDollars = InputBox("How many Dollars to the Pound?")
    PoundsGiven = txtPounds
    lblDollars.Caption = PoundsGiven * NumberOfDollars
End Sub
```

1.12 The For ... Next loop

One of the most common tasks a computer program has to perform is to repeat a set of instructions over and over again. Usually the set of instructions has to be repeated because the information being processed is a list of data each piece of which has to be dealt with in turn.

For example, the data could be a list of names or a series of numbers. Let us say that the list of data is a series of scores. The program will take each score in turn and apply the same set of instructions to process each score. The set of instructions may have the job of keeping a running total so that later on in the program an average can be calculated.

A project to calculate averages

The project

Let us imagine that your school or college has organised a sports day, and five houses or teams are involved. There are to be ten competitors in each competing team. The appointed scorer needs to know the average score for each team after all the competitors have participated. The scorer plans to use a computer to work out the results.

If the scorer were *not* using a computer, he or she would write down the score for each competitor in turn and add that score to the total score so far for the particular team. The scorer would need to do that ten times because there are ten competitors. After the tenth score has been dealt with, the average score could be calculated by dividing the total by ten.

To write a computer program for the scorer, you need a plan that sets out in steps how to create running totals and averages. First consider how to find the total of the scores for each team using pen and paper:

1   Write down zero (0, the total so far!).

2   For each competitor ...

3   ... add the competitor's score to the total.

4   Write down the result (the total score so far).

5   Get the next score (that is, go back and repeat from step 2).

6   ... ...

To work out the average score for each team, you divide the total score by the number of competitors, which is 10 in this case.

From the steps written above it becomes clear after a time that the same process is being repeated over and over again. In computing this is often called **looping**. In programming, this ability to loop is very useful because it gets the job done quicker and more efficiently. Let's now see how looping is done in Visual Basic.

Planning the looping structure

How exactly can we plan a looping structure that will get the computer to work out all the averages just as we did on paper? Figure 1.68 shows a way – not yet done in Visual Basic, but as a diagram that we will later turn into Visual Basic.

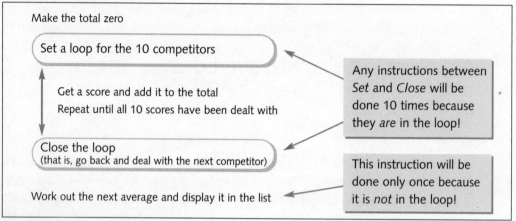

Figure 1.68 The written plan for the project

Planning the program

This will be our program plan:

1 Make the total zero (0).

2 For 10 scores ...

3 ... get a score from the keyboard, and

4 ... add the score to the total.

5 Get the next score.

6 Divide the total by 10 to find the average.

7 Display the average score in a label.

Before we get down to coding the instructions in Visual Basic, we shall create the form and objects needed for this project.

Plan for the human–computer interface (HCI)

Here is the plan:

1 create a **label** to hold the average for the house

2 create two **command buttons**, one to find the average, the other to end the program

3 create a second **label** as a title for the form.

Now that we have a plan for the form, create it as in Figure 1.69. Make sure the labels are placed exactly as you see in this design, with Label2 above Label1.

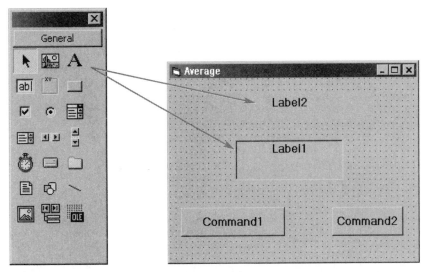

Figure 1.69 Create your form to look like this

Now apply **properties** to the objects as you have learned earlier, to achieve the result shown in Figure 1.70.

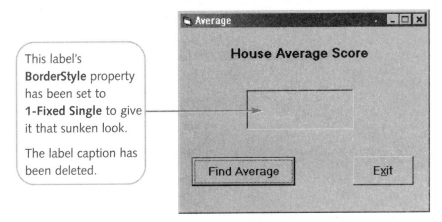

This label's **BorderStyle** property has been set to **1-Fixed Single** to give it that sunken look.

The label caption has been deleted.

Figure 1.70 The improved HCI with properties applied to the objects

Writing the program

Plan for the *Average* button

1 Make the total zero (0).

2 For 10 scores …

3 … get a score from the keyboard, and

4 … add the score to the total.

5 Get the next score.

6 Divide the total by 10 to find the average.

7 Display the average score in a label.

We will try to describe this plan using a structure diagram. In Figure 1.71 you can see how to show a loop structure using this method of design.

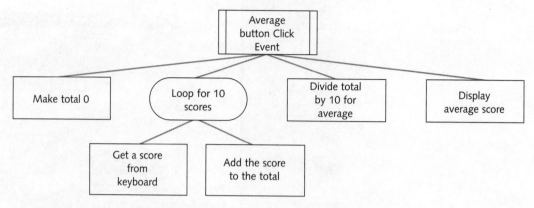

Figure 1.71 The structure diagram of the plan for the **Average** button

Code for the Average button

This is the required code:

```
Total = 0
For Competitor = 1 To 10
    Score = InputBox("Please enter the score for this competitor.")
    Total = Total + Score
Next Competitor
Average = Total / 10
Label1.Caption = Average
```

Double-click the button to bring up its code window and type those instructions into its click event.

Plan for the *Exit* button

The Exit button is to stop the program.

Code for the *Exit* button

Double-click the button to bring up its code window. Type the instruction **End** into it, as you have done in earlier projects (e.g. Figure 1.63).

Running and testing the program

Before you run the program, have a list of ten scores for which you know the average. Run the program and every time that the input box (**InputBox**) appears type in one of the ten scores.

When all ten scores have been entered, Visual Basic will display the average in the centre label.

Remember that the program has calculated the average for only one team. To calculate the averages for the other teams, the **Find Average** button will need to be clicked again by the user and the next ten scores entered in the same way.

Jargon buster

Control variable – When you use a **For … Next** loop the control variable is the variable that comes after the **For** keyword. Whenever the loop loops, the control variable either increases in value (*increments*) or decreases in value (*decrements*). To make the control variable decrease in value by one each time, as in a rocket launch countdown, the Visual Basic code would look like this:

```
For CountDown = 10 To 1 Step -1
MsgBox "Blast off in " & CountDown & " seconds."
Next CountDown
MsgBox "We have blast off!"
```

The **Step** keyword tells Visual Basic the amount that the control variable has to come down by each time.

Understanding the For … Next loop

Read again through the Visual Basic code we have used for looping with a For … Next loop. Make sure you understand each line of code. The explanations are given below in square brackets. *Try to understand what's going on in this loop even if you have to read this explanation several times.*

> Total = 0

[**Total** is first set to zero.]

> **For** Competitor = 1 To 10

[Then the computer has to go round a loop ten times. Each time round the loop, the variable **Competitor** – called the *control variable* – is used to keep track of how often the computer has looped. The value of *competitor* is increased by 1 each time.]

[The next two instructions inside the **For … Next** loop are acted on ten times. Every time around the loop the computer asks for the next score.]

> Score = InputBox("Please enter the score for this competitor.")
> Total = Total + Score

[**Total** gets an updated value each time round the loop – that is, its old value plus the last **Score** fetched.]

> Next Competitor

[At this point in the code, if the loop has still not been repeated ten times the processing loops back to the **For** line and repeats what is inside the loop.]

> Average = Total / 10

[Once the loop has been done ten times the **Average** is calculated by dividing **Total** by 10. *We are no longer in the loop.*]

> Label1.Caption = Average

[The average is displayed in **Label1** as a caption.]

The user then needs to click the **Find average** button again to find the average score for the next team, and so on for each team.

Now you try

Design a form and write a program that asks for marks gained in six subjects. The program should display the total of the marks and the average of the six marks. Make use of a **For ... Next** loop and **Label** objects to display the results.

 ## Now you try

Use the ideas from the sports day program you created to help you carry out the following task. You will need to start a new project.

Design an HCI and a program that works like a cash register in a shop and displays in a list box the separate amounts that make up the total of the bill for the customer. The program should ask for three amounts and then total the bill. See below for some pointers. When you have succeeded in that task, modify the code so that it can deal with six amounts.

Think about the steps that the program will have to take:

- You will need to set a total to zero first.
- How often will you have to loop?
- Get an amount from the user (an input box?).
- Make sure you keep a running total. How was that done in the sports day program?
- Display the amount in the list box. How do you add an item to a list box?
- You need to close the loop so that the program can loop back.
- When you are out of the loop you can display the total for the bill in a label.

Look at the screen shots in Figure 1.72 to get an idea of what you are aiming to achieve.

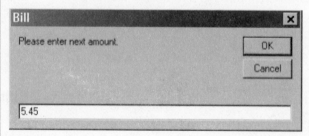

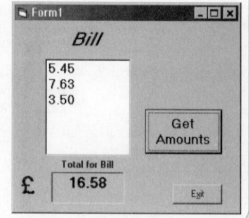

Figure 1.72 Hints for the supertask

What did you learn?

Creating forms and user-friendly interfaces

(*List boxes*)

- You can create a **list box** and **command buttons**.
- To show the properties for a control, you press **F4**.
- The Properties window is used a lot to change the properties of controls: the **Caption** property for buttons and labels, the **Font** property for buttons, labels and text boxes, the **Text** property for text boxes, and **BorderStyle** for a label to give it that sunken look.
- You know how to display names in a list box using the **AddItem** method.
- You can set a list box to display in alphabetical order by setting its **Sort** property in the Properties window.
- You know how to save your form and your project.
- You press **F5** to run the program in Visual Basic.

Documenting your program

(*Rem and ' (apostrophe)*)

- The ' (apostrophe) and **Rem** let you put comments into the body of your program code. You can include comments about the author of the program, the date and what the program is supposed to do.
- You can use **MsgBox** to put messages on the screen. For example:

      MsgBox "This program will display a list of names."

- You can print the program code from the **File** menu.
- Alt + PrintScreen keys are used to get a shot of the screen when the program is running.

Entering data

(*InputBox*)

- If you want to get data into the computer from your program, use **InputBox**. For example:

      FriendsName = InputBox("Please enter a name.")

- FriendsName is an example of a **variable**. The contents of a variable can change during the running of a program.
- List1.**Clear** will clear a list box.
- List1.**RemoveItem** List1.**ListCount** −1 removes the last item in a list.
- List1.**RemoveItem** List1.**ListIndex** removes only the item the user has highlighted in the list box.

Doing arithmetic

(*Calculations*)

- You know the symbols the computer uses to do arithmetic: +, -, *, and /.
- You can create shapes for the arithmetic symbols with the line and shape tool.
- Use the function **Val** if you want to do arithmetic with values put in a text box.

- You know how to avoid the **overflow error**.
- You can put an arithmetic result in a label. For example:

      Label1.Caption = Val(Text1) + Val(Text2)

- You know that it is important to type the commands in Visual Basic precisely. Otherwise Visual Basic will not understand what it has to do, and will come up with an error when you run a program.

Creating totals and averages with For ... Next loops

- You now have a basic knowledge of **For ... Next** loops and why they are used.
- You can write a program to create a running total and calculate an average for scores.
- You were given help with a task to work out a customer bill using a list box to show the bill.

UNIT 2

2.1 Adding graphics to a form

Picture this

The form that the user sees is very important. It allows interaction and communication between what the program is trying to achieve and the actions of the user. Enhancing the appearance of the form with pictures and other graphical elements can improve the interaction and communication. In all your projects you should be trying to make the user's experience enjoyable and your programs user-friendly.

You will learn to use a new Visual Basic control called a **PictureBox** that allows you to display pictures of different types. Adding graphics to a form is very easy.

Ice cream comes in many flavours. The next project involves showing three different pictures of ice cream when certain buttons are clicked.

Creating the human–computer interface (HCI)

Start a new project and place a **PictureBox** control on the form, as in Figure 2.1. Make sure it is selected and press **F4** and set its **Autosize** property to True, as in Figure 2.2.

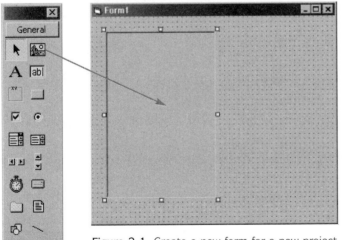

Figure 2.1 Create a new form for a new project

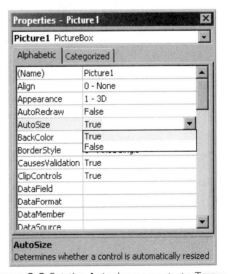

Figure 2.2 Set the **Autosize** property to True

Next set its **Picture** property to a picture file that exists on your hard disk, by clicking the ellipsis button shown in Figure 2.3. This will allow you to browse your disk or other backing storage device for the file you need. Open the Icecream1 file that you will find on your Visual Basic CD that comes with the book.

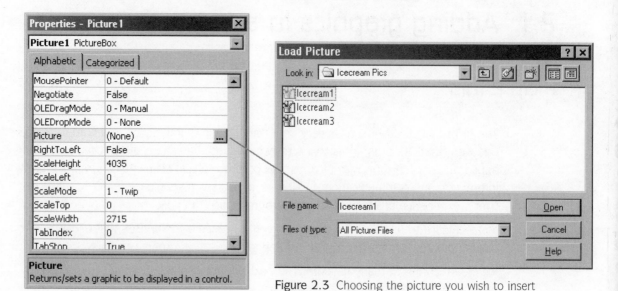

Figure 2.3 Choosing the picture you wish to insert

If you successfully managed to open the picture file your form should now look like the left part of Figure 2.4.

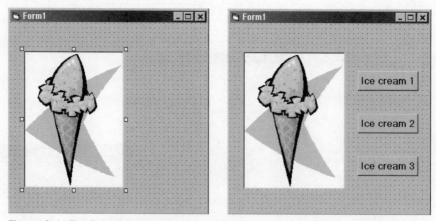

Figure 2.4 The first picture appears on the form, and buttons have been added

Next add three buttons to the form, as you learned in Unit 1. Change the captions and font sizes for the buttons. The font is bold 12pt in the right part of Figure 2.4.

That completes the design for the form. At least when you run the program the **Picture1** box will not be empty to start with.

You will now program the buttons so that they display other ice cream pictures.

Writing the program

Plan for the *Ice cream 1* button

The plan is to get an ice cream picture from the CD-ROM and place it into **Picture1**.

Code for the *Ice cream 1* button

The code you will need for the buttons at runtime is no more than one line:

```
Picture1 = LoadPicture("c:\My Pictures\Icecream1.bmp")
```

The *path* shown here will have to correspond with where the picture file is on your hard drive.

Double-click the button to bring up its code window and type the line of code into its click event, as in the top part of Figure 2.5. You will have to make sure that the file you point to here does exist in this location.

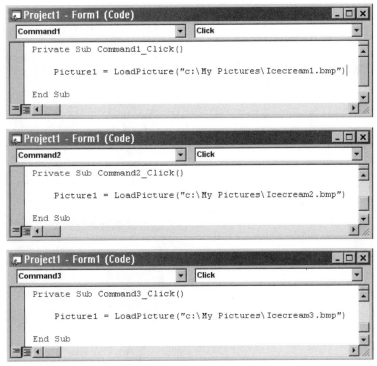

Figure 2.5 The code windows for the three buttons

Plan for the *Ice cream 2* and *3* buttons

As for the first button, the plan is to get two further ice cream pictures and place them into **Picture1**.

Code for the *Ice cream 2* and *3* buttons

For each of the two further buttons, double-click the buttons in turn to get their code windows and type the lines of code into their click events, as in the middle and bottom parts of Figure 2.5. The code lines are:

```
Picture1 = LoadPicture("c:\My Pictures\Icecream2.bmp")
```
and
```
Picture1 = LoadPicture("c:\My Pictures\Icecream3.bmp")
```

Running and testing the program

Press **F5** to run the program, and correct any errors that may appear. The most likely error to occur is that Visual Basic cannot find the picture files. Ensure that the location of the picture files corresponds to the path that you specify in the program.

Jargon buster

Path – A path is a set of directions that lets the operating system's filing system know where to find a file on the computer's hard drive or other backing store. For example, the code "c:\My Pictures\Icecream1.bmp" tells the filing system that the Icecream1.bmp file is in a folder called My Pictures on the C drive. Note that the path has to be typed in quotes. The colon after the drive letter and the backslash between folders and filename are also necessary for the syntax.

Figure 2.6 shows the pictures that your program should load into the **PictureBox** when the different buttons are clicked.

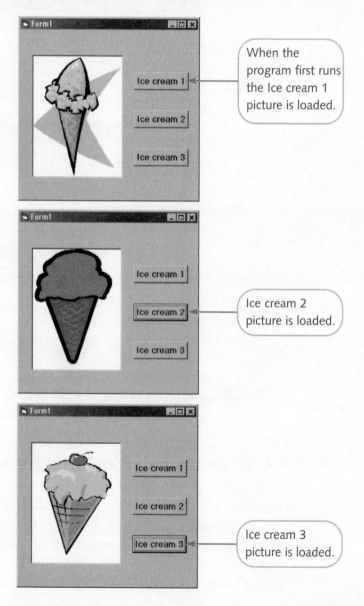

When the program first runs the Ice cream 1 picture is loaded.

Ice cream 2 picture is loaded.

Ice cream 3 picture is loaded.

Figure 2.6
The result of clicking each of the three buttons

Runtime or system errors

A **runtime** or **system** error is a mistake in a program that causes the computer to stop unexpectedly during processing. Runtime errors occur when a program encounters an outside event, or an undiscovered syntax error causes a program to stop running.

Trouble with file names

Visual Basic will throw up an error if, for example, a filename is misspelled or a file you specify in a path does not physically exist on the hard drive or on an accessible disk (a floppy disk or CD-ROM). For example, the program instruction

```
Picture1 = LoadPicture("c:\My Pictures\Icecream1.bmp")
```

commands that the file **Icecream1.bmp** be placed into a picture box **Picture1**. If the file happens not to be in the folder **My Pictures** on the hard disk (C:) then a system error will occur. The top part of Figure 2.7 shows an error message that might appear when this happens. The file is not there or you may have misspelled the name of the file. What do you do?

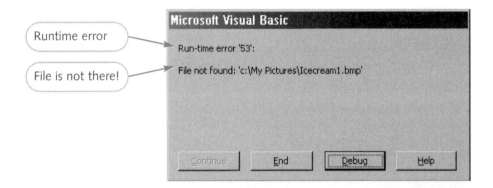

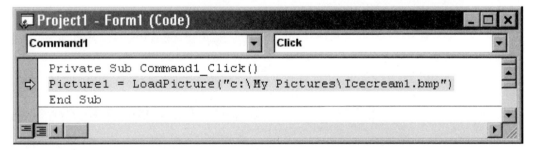

Figure 2.7 A Visual Basic error message, and the result of clicking the Debug button

If you click **End** the program will stop and you can then try finding the error yourself and debug the program. Correct the error when you find it.

Alternatively, if you click **Debug** on the error message box Visual Basic will pinpoint the error by highlighting it, as in the bottom part of Figure 2.7. In this case the program is still running but paused. You may be able to correct the error right away and then press **F5** and continue running the program. If you change your mind about correcting the program, choose **End** from the **Run** menu.

Trouble with folder names

If the specified folder does not exist on your hard drive, or if you have misspelled it, you will get a runtime error message as in the top part of Figure 2.8. The folder is not there or you may have misspelled its name. What do you do this time?

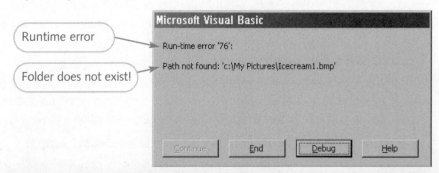

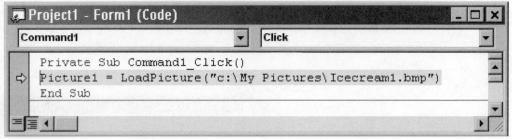

Figure 2.8 Another Visual Basic error message, and the result of clicking the Debug button

If you click **End** the program will stop and you can then try debugging the program as you did before. Find the mistake in the code and correct it. If you click on **Debug** then Visual Basic will pinpoint the error by highlighting it for you, as in the bottom part of Figure 2.8. Again the program is still running but paused. Once more you may be able to correct the error right away and then press **F5** and continue running the program. If you change your mind about correcting the program, choose **End** from the **Run** menu.

Visual Basic help

Visual Basic will always offer on-line help, so be sure to try **Help** if you are really stuck. In this case clicking **Help** will not offer much assistance with the 'Path not found' topic. However, for the 'File was not found' error, **Help** explains the reason for the error with the screen shown in Figure 2.9.

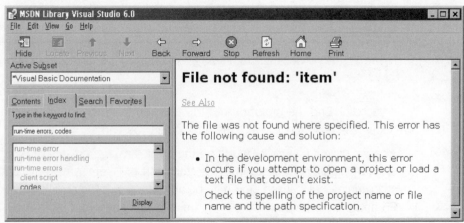

Figure 2.9 A Visual Basic help screen

 Now you try

Design a form and write a program for the following task. Create a project that has a **picture box** *and* a **list box** on the form.

- Use the picture box to display pictures of flags of various countries.
- Decide on a favourite sport of yours and use the list box to display the names of a team.

When the user clicks a button for a country or team, the flag for that country is to be displayed in the picture box and the names of the players appear in the list box.

The project when run should look like the screenshots in Figure 2.10.

Figure 2.10 The intended result of running the program

You could use the ice cream project in this chapter to help you get started. However, if you start a new project remember to set PictureBox's **Autosize** property to true.

Make sure you have the pictures of the flags you want to use in a folder for which you know the path. For example, the path **C:\My Flags\BrazilFlag.bmp** would need to have a folder created on the **C drive** called **My Flags** where the pictures of the flags are located.

If you are connected to a network at school or college, ask your teacher for the drive letter to your home directory. So, for example, if your home directory is **H** then you could create a folder called **My Flags** on the **H drive** and move the pictures of your flags into it. Your path would then be: **H:\My Flags\NameOfFlag.bmp**, where NameOfFlag is the name of the file on your drive.

You will find some more flags on the CD-ROM that comes with the book.

2.2 Do ... Loop Until

Password check

Earlier you learned how to use the **For ... Next** loop. You know that loops are used in programming to repeat a set of instructions. However, the For ... Next loop is useful for repeating instructions only if the programmer knows beforehand the number of times the loop will need to be repeated. It is often *not* known how many times a repetition will be required.

For example, in a program that asks for a password it is not known beforehand how often the user might have to type in the password before the program will accept it. We need a different type of loop that can deal with this sort of situation. The user may have forgotten the password and has to try several times before it is accepted.

A **Do … Loop Until** loop can be used when it is not known how often the program will have to loop. The way this type of loop works is like this:

- **Do** (ask for a password)
- **Loop Until** (the correct password is typed).

Visual Basic will keep asking for the password until the correct one is typed. The instruction line between the **Do** and **Loop Until** is repeated until the true condition is met at the **Loop Until** line.

This is known as a **conditional loop** because a condition has to be met before the loop can be exited.

The next project involves a program to repeatedly ask for a password until the correct password is entered. A message is to be displayed when the correct password is entered.

Creating the human–computer interface (HCI)

1 Create two labels to prompt a password from the user when the form is clicked.

2 Use one label for a title to the form and the other label to tell the user what to do.

3 The *form's* click event will hold the Visual Basic instructions to check the password.

4 Set the form's caption to **Password Entry**. To change the form's caption carry out the following steps:

- Click the form. Ensure it is the form that you click and not an object on it.
- Press **F4** to get its Properties window.
- In the Properties window set the form's caption to **Password Entry** (Figure 2.11).

Next place a button to exit the program. The form should look like Figure 2.12 when you have finished designing it.

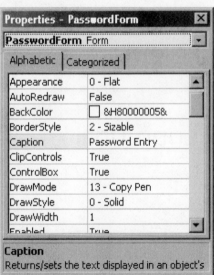

Figure 2.11 Setting the form's caption

Figure 2.12 How your form will look

Writing the program

Plan for the form's click event

1 Do.

2 Ask for a password.

3 **Loop Until** 'Let me in' is typed.

4 Display the message 'You have clearance'.

Code for the form's click event

The required code is:

```
Do
    ID = InputBox("Please enter your password.")
Loop Until ID = "Let me in"
MsgBox "You have Clearance"
```

Double-click the form to open its code window and type this code into its click event procedure, as in Figure 2.13. Make sure the **Click** event for the form is showing (arrowed).

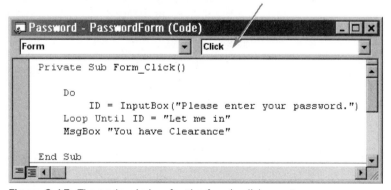

Figure 2.13 The code window for the form's click event

Code for the *Exit* button

As you have seen many times now, the code for the **Exit** button is simply

```
End
```

Type that command in the button's click event window.

Running and testing the program

Run the program by pressing **F5**. When you are asked for a password, type 'Let me in' (without the quotes). Make sure you type the password exactly as specified in the code, otherwise the program will keep looping! Also type in a *wrong* password to test that the loop is operating correctly. When the correct password is typed the message 'You have Clearance' should be displayed.

Figure 2.14 shows the program running.

Figure 2.14 The form and the dialogue box with the program running

Understanding the Do ... Loop Until loop

Read again through the Visual Basic code we have used for looping with a Do ... Loop Until loop. Make sure you understand each line of code. The explanations are given below in square brackets.

```
Do
```

[The **Do** tells Visual Basic to start the loop.]

```
ID = InputBox("Please enter your password.")
```

[**ID** is the variable that will hold whatever the user types into the **InputBox**.]

```
Loop Until ID = "Let me in"
```

[This line closes the loop and Visual Basic tests what the variable **ID** holds. The condition set is that **ID** should hold **Let me in**. If the variable holds that phrase then the loop is exited and processing carries on at the next line. If the variable holds any other phrase then Visual Basic loops back to the **Do** line.]

```
MsgBox "You have Clearance"
```

[This line will be done only when the password is correct. Visual Basic will display the message **You have Clearance**.]

Now you try

Design a project that uses a **Do ... Loop Until** to ask a quiz question and which will keep asking the question until the user types in the right answer. The program should display a message that says 'Correct' when the right answer is given.

2.3 Using Dim

Finding maximum and minimum values

We often need to find the greatest or smallest value in a list of numbers. For example, at an athletics meeting the electronic scoreboard needs to be updated with the times and distances for many competitors. To be able to know if any records have been broken it is necessary to work out what the minimum and maximum values are for different events, whether they be times or distances. The minimum and maximum values are compared with records set at other events to find out if new records can be awarded. Some lists can be very long and it would take too long to work out by hand.

Computers are very good and quick at this task. All you have to do is type in the numbers or gather them electronically from around the track and field and the computer will do the rest.

You will learn in this chapter how to create a project to find the minimum and maximum heights of people in your class.

For this project you will open an existing project that is on your CD-ROM for the book. The project is called 'Heights' and you will find it in a folder called **Heights**. This project has the code that will do the calculations for finding the minimum and maximum values. The code instructions for this are in a couple of procedures called **MinNo** and **MaxNo**. They will be discussed later in the chapter, and there is further information on procedures in the document called 'Using procedures' on your CD-ROM.

Creating the human–computer interface (HCI)

When you open the project, the form will appear as in Figure 2.15.

Figure 2.15 The opening form for the project

Creating the form

1 Create a **list box** and change its font style and size to bold 14pt.

2 Place **labels** 1 and 2 where you see them in Figure 2.16. Their font style and size are bold and 12pt. Also set their **BorderStyle** to 1 – Fixed Single to give them that sunken look.

3 You will need two **buttons**, so create them. Change their **Name** properties to **cmdEnterHeights** and **cmdExit**. Their captions should be **Enter Heights** and **Exit** respectively. To change the **Name** of a button follow these steps:

   • Make sure it is selected by clicking on it.
   • Press **F4** to get its Property window and set its **Name** to **cmdEnterHeights**.
   • Repeat those two steps for the second button, setting its **Name** property to **cmdExit**.

4 Create a **Label** to act as a title to the list box by changing its caption to **Heights**.

When you have finished designing the form it should look like Figure 2.16. After the various properties have been set it should look like Figure 2.17.

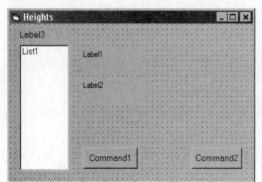
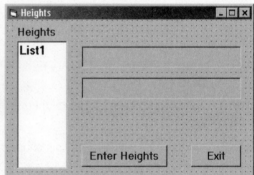

Figure 2.16 The basic form

Figure 2.17 The form with all the properties set

Writing the program

In this program you will learn to create a procedure that you will be able to use in the **Enter Heights** button.

You also have to tell Visual Basic how long the list is going to be that will hold the numbers. You will learn how to do this by using the Visual Basic keyword **Dim**, which is short for 'dimension'. When you dimension space in memory in Visual Basic it means that you set it aside for the program. The program then uses the space to hold the list. You must also give the list a variable name so that you can refer to it in Visual Basic code within the program.

Jargon buster

Calling – Programmers talk about *calling* a procedure. This does not mean that the procedure is given a name but that Visual Basic is told to go and look for the procedure and carry out the instructions in it. So what you will be doing is calling the procedure from the **Enter Heights** button.

Plan for the *GetHeights* procedure

1 Allocate room in memory for the list.

2 Take in the list of heights.

3 Find and display the heights in a List box.

4 Find and display the maximum height in Label1.

5 Find and display the minimum height in Label2.

> You can view the structure diagram version of this plan on your CD-ROM.

Code for the *GetHeights* procedure

As was mentioned earlier, the button **Enter Heights** calls a procedure **GetHeights**. Before you can type the code into the **GetHeights** procedure you have to create the procedure. To create the procedure, follow these steps.

Double-click the form to open a code window. From the **Tools** menu select **Add Procedure**. Type the name of the procedure (GetHeights) into the name box, as in Figure 2.18, and leave the other options in the dialogue box as shown. Click **OK**. A procedure called **GetHeights** is created.

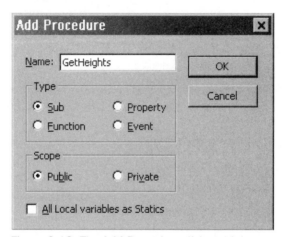

> You should read the section on Using procedures on your CD-ROM.

Figure 2.18 The **Add Procedure** dialogue box

In the code window make sure that the name of the procedure is showing. Then type the following code into the procedure as in Figure 2.19:

```
Dim Heights(10)
TakeInNumbers Heights( ), 10
MaxNo Heights( ), 10
MinNo Heights( ), 10
```

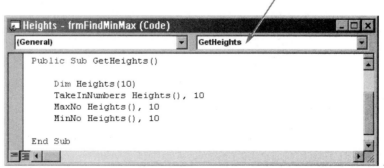

Figure 2.19 The code window for the **GetHeights** procedure

It is important that the code instructions are typed exactly as you see above, otherwise your program will fail. Make sure that when you type the code you don't miss out the brackets after the list names, and it is also important that the commas are not missed out either. Later in the chapter you will see in detail what is happening in the code.

Jargon buster

Procedures and Subs – Visual Basic has been developed from earlier versions of the language Basic, where **sub**routines was the name given to what we now call procedures. The keyword **Sub** for declaring a procedure was therefore kept for compatibility reasons.

Code modules – A module is the Visual Basic term for a library of procedures or functions. A **code module** is used to store procedures or functions that are intended for reuse in one project or over a number of projects across multiple forms and modules. The procedures and functions in a module will be of a similar kind. For example you might create a module to hold just procedures that ask for numerical input and another module that has procedures that deal with text input. A code module when saved is saved with a **.bas** three-letter extension (e.g. Heights.bas).

Form module – Visual Basic also lets you create procedures and functions in a form module. In fact the procedure **GetHeights** that you created in this chapter was created at the form level so it is a form module procedure. Form level procedures or functions cannot be shared outside the form in which they are created. To share a procedure and be able to use it in another project, it has to be placed in a code module and the module subsequently added into your project.

Public – The keyword **Public** that Visual Basic insists in placing in front of **Sub** in the declaration of a procedure or function has to do with where the procedure can be called from, or its **scope**. There is also a keyword **Private** that restricts the use of the procedure or function to the module in which it is created. You can easily ignore both at this stage of your programming experience.

Plan for the *Enter Heights* button

The plan is to call the procedure **GetHeights**.

Code for the *Enter Heights* button

Double-click the button to bring up its code window. Type this line of code into the button's code window, as in Figure 2.20:

```
GetHeights
```

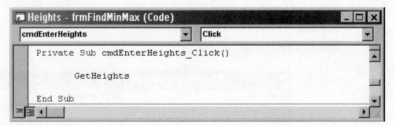

Figure 2.20 The code window for the **GetHeights** click event

Code for the *Exit* button

As before, the code for the **Exit** button is simply

```
End
```

Type that command in the button's click event window.

Running and testing the program

Before you run the program prepare the data that you are going to input. Collect ten heights from members of your class. The heights should be entered in feet – so 5ft 6in would be entered as 5.50. Here is a table to help you with the decimal values for feet and inches:

4ft 1in	4.08	4ft 11in	4.92	5ft 9in	5.75
4ft 2in	4.17	5ft 0in	5.00	5ft 10in	5.83
4ft 3in	4.25	5ft 1in	5.08	5ft 11in	5.92
4ft 4in	4.33	5ft 2in	5.17	6ft 0in	6.00
4ft 5in	4.42	5ft 3in	5.25	6ft 1in	6.08
4ft 6in	4.50	5ft 4in	5.33	6ft 2in	6.17
4ft 7in	4.58	5ft 5in	5.42	6ft 3in	6.25
4ft 8in	4.67	5ft 6in	5.50	6ft 4in	6.33
4ft 9in	4.75	5ft 7in	5.58	6ft 5in	6.42
4ft 10in	4.83	5ft 8in	5.67	6ft 6in	6.50

The program will first ask for ten heights, as in Figure 2.21. The program will add each height to the list box as you type them in.

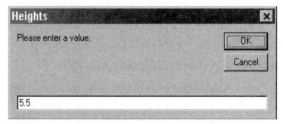

Figure 2.21 The input HCI

When the heights have all been entered the program will calculate the maximum and minimum values and display them in the labels, as in Figure 2.22. Notice that a **scroll bar** has been added by Visual Basic because there is not enough space to list all the ten numbers at once.

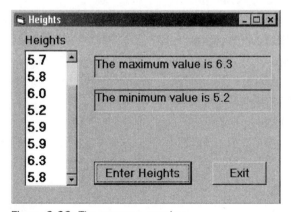

Figure 2.22 The program running

Save your project when you have it working correctly.

Jargon buster

Lists and arrays – In this chapter we have talked about the procedures **MinNo** and **MaxNo** handling lists. Here we are not talking about a list box but a different type of list which programmers more commonly call an **array**. In Chapters 3.3 and 3.4 we will go into detail about arrays. For the moment just remember that Visual Basic requires that we set aside space in memory with **Dim** if we want to use them with these two library procedures, **MinNo** and **MaxNo**.

Understanding the GetHeights procedure

Read again through the Visual Basic code we have used for the GetHeights procedure. Make sure you understand each line of code. The explanations are given below in square brackets.

Public Sub GetHeights()

[This line tells Visual Basic where the procedure begins.]

Dim Heights(10)

[Here room is set aside in the computer's memory to hold the list **Heights**. The number in brackets allocates room for ten items. **Dim** is the keyword that Visual Basic understands for setting aside memory. When you use **Dim**, Visual Basic knows you want to create a list.]

TakeInNumbers Heights(), 10

[When you opened the project for this chapter, **TakeInNumbers** was one of the procedures included in the project. It was written to help you get the numbers into the computer. Note that the programmer must pass the list to the procedure along with the number of items it can hold. The procedure can then fill it with the numbers.]

MaxNo Heights(), 10

[**MaxNo** is a procedure that finds the maximum value in a list of numbers. The list has to be passed to the procedure along with the number of items it can hold. The procedure will also display the maximum value in **Label1**.]

MinNo Heights(), 10

[**MinNo** is a procedure that finds the minimum value in a list of numbers. The list has to be passed to the procedure along with the number of items it can hold. The procedure will also display the minimum value in **Label2**.]

End Sub

[Tells Visual Basic that the **GetHeights** procedure ends here.]

Now you try

Alter the program you have designed in this unit so that the caption above **List1** changes depending on the group of people or objects for which you are finding the highest and smallest values. You will need to set the caption for **Label3** at runtime (while the program is running) by asking the user to input (use **InputBox**) the name of the group he or she wants to deal with. Remember **Label3.Caption** can be set to hold what the user types in.

Setting a label's caption at runtime is straightforward. For example:

```
Label3.Caption = VariableName
```

would set the label's caption to whatever the **VariableName** happens to hold.

You will have to decide where you will insert the code to ask for the group that is being dealt with and set **Label3** to whatever the user enters.

Figures 2.23 and 2.24 will give you a few pointers.

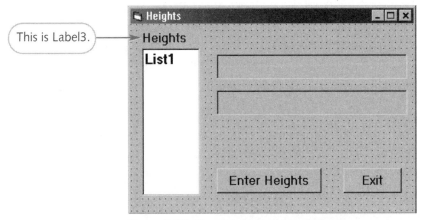

This is Label3.

Figure 2.23 The HCI for the extended task

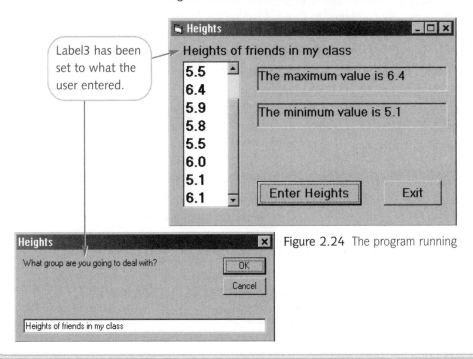

Label3 has been set to what the user entered.

Figure 2.24 The program running

You have already created a program for a sports day scorer to obtain an average score for each house team. As the program stands, the scorer has to click the **Find Average** button every time the scores for a new house team have to be averaged. The previous averages are then lost.

What you will do in this chapter is improve the usefulness of the program by getting it to ask for the number of houses the scorer wants to deal with. The program will alert the user that it is ready to deal with the next set of scores. You will have to learn how to make use of *nested* **For ... Next loops** so that the program does not stop after just one house team. The HCI for the program will also need to be changed, as it will have to display more than one average score. Label objects will be no use in this case for display purposes for the average scores, as we cannot guess in advance how many houses might be involved. We will use a list box that can deal with any number of average scores to display the results.

Let us remind ourselves of the steps that are involved in finding an average score for one house (remember we could write this down on paper):

1 Write down zero (0, the total so far!).

2 For each competitor ...

3 ... add the competitor's score to the total.

4 Write down the result (the total score so far).

5 Get the next score (that is, go back and repeat from step 2).

6 ... ...

These steps – let us not forget – deal only with one house team. What would we have to do to get the computer to process the scores for the other house teams? Yes, we need to repeat the same set of instructions for any number of houses! What we need to do is **loop** and **nest** this set of instructions within an **outer** loop. We already have an **inner** loop that deals with a set of ten scores. Diagrammatically what we require is shown in Figure 2.25.

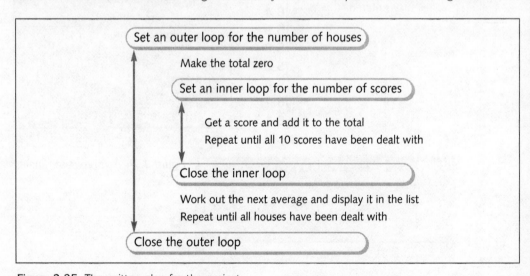

Figure 2.25 The written plan for the project

Creating the human–computer interface (HCI)

1 Create two command buttons with name properties **cmdFindAverages** and **cmdExit**, and with captions **Find Averages** and **Exit**.

2 Create a list box to hold the averages and give it the name property **lstScores**.

3 Create a label to title the form **House Average Scores**, and caption the form **Improved Sports**.

The form when designed should look like Figure 2.26.

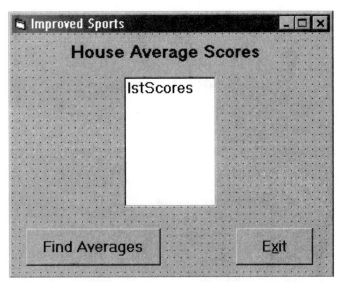

Figure 2.26 The HCI for the sports day project

Writing the program

Plan for the *Find Averages* button

1 Ask the user how many house teams there will be.

2 Set an *outer* For … Next loop for the number of houses to input.

3 Set the total back to zero.

4 Give the user a message that the next house team will now be dealt with.

5 Set an *inner* For … Next loop to deal with a set of ten scores.

6 Input a score.

7 Update the total so far.

8 End the *inner* loop.

9 Work out the average for this set of scores (the total divided by 10).

10 Display the average for this set in the list box with AddItem.

11 End the *outer* loop.

Code for the *Find Averages* button

The required code is:

```
Sub cmdFindAverages_Click()
NoOfHouses = InputBox("How many houses are taking part?")
For House = 1 To NoOfHouses
    Total = 0
    MsgBox "Ready for next House?"
    For competitor = 1 To 10
        Score = InputBox("Please enter the score for this competitor.")
        Total = Total + Score
    Next competitor
    Average = Total / 10
    lstScores.AddItem Average
Next House
End Sub
```

Double-click the **Find Averages** button to bring up its code window and type this code into its click event procedure, as in Figure 2.27.

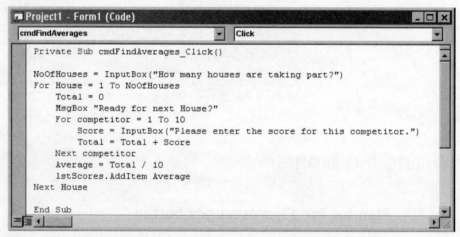

Figure 2.27 The code window for the Find Averages button

Code for the *Exit* button

As before, the code for the **Exit** button is simply

```
End
```

Type that command in the button's click event window.

Running and testing the program

When you have typed the code into the buttons, run your program and test it. Write down a set of test data for a number of house teams and work out by hand what each average should be. Now type in the same data into the program and compare the two results.

Make sure your program is producing the correct results. Is it asking for the number of houses now? Are the averages OK? Is the list box displaying the averages?

Save your project as '**Improved Sports**'. You will need it for further development in the task below.

Now you try

Your task is to produce an an enhanced version of the project **Improved Sports** that has *two* list boxes. The new list box should hold the names of the house teams that participated at the sports day.

Open the project you saved above and add the extra list box and add the extra lines of code that you will need into the **Find Averages** button. The extra instructions will include getting the names of the house teams from the user and displaying them in the new list box.

Figure 2.28 shows a runtime screen display of such an enhanced version of the project, and yours should look similar. Five houses have been processed in this case. The program has obtained the names of the houses from the user and displayed them in the new list box.

Figure 2.28 The enhanced program running

Jargon buster

Object Name Prefix – It is good programming practice to give the variables you use sensible and meaningful names, and when you use an object's name in code you should apply the same rule. So, for example, if you have a text box on a form that accepts the entry of the name of a team, you might want to name the text box **TeamEntry** and use it in code within your program. When you look back at your code at a later date you may not remember that TeamEntry in fact refers to a text box and you might try to use it as a parameter to a procedure. *That would not work.* As an aid to making program code more readable, objects that are used can have a prefix added to the start of the name. TeamName could be given the prefix **txt** so that it becomes **txtTeamName**.

There is an agreed *standard of name prefixes* for objects in the Visual Basic Toolbox. The more common ones are:

- **cmd**   CommandButton
- **txt**   TextBox
- **lbl**   Label
- **lst**   ListBox
- **pic**   PictureBox.

Use a prefix for objects whenever you think it will help you to make your code more readable.

2.5 If ... Then

The computer making decisions

A Geography teacher has heard that you are learning to program using Visual Basic. She asks whether you could write a program that she can use with her pupils to help them with their Geography. She needs a program that asks a question and the pupil then has to select from a menu of five possible answers. The program also needs to tell the pupil whether the answer is correct or wrong.

The description of the project implies that the program will have to make decisions on the basis of what the user inputs. *If* the user inputs the correct answer *then* the computer should display 'Correct', but *if* the user enters the wrong answer *then* the computer should display 'Wrong'.

You should make use of a **combo box**. This is like a list box except that the user can pull the list down as a pull-down menu. A combo box can be obtained from the Visual Basic Toolbox, as shown in Figure 2.29.

Use this control to create a combo box.

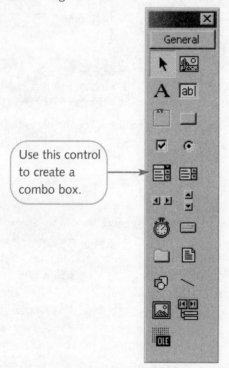

Figure 2.29 The combo box icon on the Visual Basic Toolbox

A combo box is useful because it takes up less room on the form. The list it hides is on display only when the user pulls the menu down.

A combo box has a display box at the top where the user's selection remains visible. You can set its **Text** property to an initial value in order to give the user a hint or *default value*. On each of the forms in Figure 2.30 you will see a combo box, and in this case the hint the user receives is 'Pick a City'.

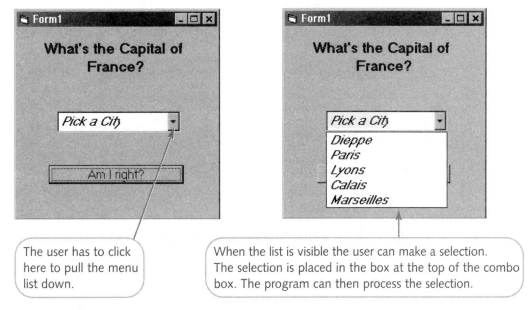

The user has to click here to pull the menu list down.

When the list is visible the user can make a selection. The selection is placed in the box at the top of the combo box. The program can then process the selection.

Figure 2.30 The **combo box** hides a list that is visible only when the user clicks on the down arrow.

Creating the human-computer interface (HCI)

1 Create a combo box (**Combo1**) to hold the menu of options. Set its **Text** property to 'Pick a City'.

2 Create a button to test the user's choice. Give it the caption **Am I right?** and a name cmdAmIRight.

3 Create a label to display the Geography question. Set its caption property to '**What is the Capital of France?**'

Writing the program

Plan for the *Form Load* procedure

The **Form Load** procedure will fill the combo box with the list of cities using the **AddItem** method that you have met before.

Code for the *Form Load* procedure

It is often necessary in Visual Basic to have some events happen when the program first runs. In this project we use the **Form Load** procedure to fill a combo box with a list of cities so that the user can make a choice. If you double-click the form in design mode you will be able to type your commands into the **Form Load** procedure:

```
Combo1.AddItem "Dieppe"
Combo1.AddItem "Paris"
Combo1.AddItem "Lyons"
Combo1.AddItem "Calais"
Combo1.AddItem "Marseilles"
```

> You can view the structure diagram version of the plan on your CD-ROM.

This is shown in the top part of Figure 2.31. The bottom part of the figure shows you what to do if the **Form Load** window is not displayed.

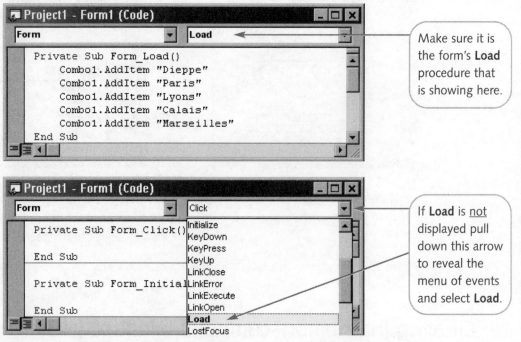

Make sure it is the form's **Load** procedure that is showing here.

If **Load** is <u>not</u> displayed pull down this arrow to reveal the menu of events and select **Load**.

Figure 2.31 The code for the Form Load procedure has been entered

Any instructions that Visual Basic finds in the **Form Load** procedure are carried out as soon as you press F5 to run your program.

Plan for the *Am I Right?* button

1 If the user's selection in the combo box is 'Paris', then display 'Correct' in a message box.

2 If the user's selection in the combo box is not 'Paris', then display 'Wrong' in a message box.

Code for the *Am I Right?* button

These two lines go into the **Am I right?** button:

```
If Combo1.Text = "Paris" Then MsgBox "Correct"
If Combo1.Text <> "Paris" Then MsgBox "Wrong"
```

Note that the two symbols '<' and '>' are used side by side (<>) to mean 'not equal to'.

Running and testing the program

Run your program and test that the message 'Correct' is displayed when 'Paris' is selected from the combo box and that the message 'Wrong' is displayed for any other choice.

Save your project as '**Geography**'.

Now you try

At this point you need to get out your atlas! Extend the **Geography** program you have just been working on and set some more questions on capital cities. Look on the Internet or find out whether there is a multimedia atlas on your system for help on the capital cities.

Look at Figure 2.32 and you will see that the form has to be a bit bigger to accommodate the extra questions. Also, rather than have message boxes popping up with 'Correct' or 'Wrong' it is a better idea to have **Labels 6 to 10** to display either 'Correct' or 'Wrong'.

Create another four combo boxes to display the lists of cities.

These labels will display either 'Correct' or 'Wrong'.

Figure 2.32 An extended form for the enhanced project

Think how you will make this simple adjustment to your coding. The coding in the **Form Load** procedure and in the **Am I right?** button's click event will require attention.

Figure 2.33 shows an example of the program running.

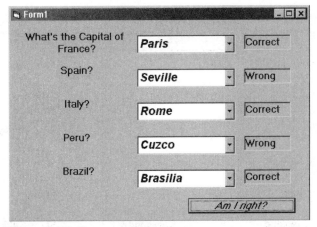

Figure 2.33 The program running

What are the options?

In many cases, programming in Visual Basic is about giving users a choice of options on a form. In older text-based programming languages the user would be presented with questions one after the other to which a keyboard response would be requested. Although this method can be simulated in Visual Basic by the use of **InputBox**, it is not the recommended way of doing things in Visual Basic.

A much more user-friendly way is to use **option buttons** (also sometimes called 'radio buttons' because older car radios used to have channel select buttons that would cancel when a new button was pressed).

You can use Visual Basic's **OptionButton** control to present a set of options to the user. A set of options buttons is treated by Visual Basic *as a group*. When the program runs only one button in a group can be selected – so it is an 'either/or' type of selection.

You will learn in this chapter how to use a set of option buttons to create a timetable of your school or college subjects.

Creating the human–computer interface (HCI)

1 Create five **option buttons** for the working days. Change their captions to the names of the days, with a bold font style.

2 Create a list box with the name **lstSubjects** that will hold a day's subjects. Set its font style to bold and italic.

3 Create two command buttons with names **cmdShowSubjects** and **cmdExit**, and with captions **Show Subjects** and **Exit**.

Figure 2.34 shows what you should be aiming to produce.

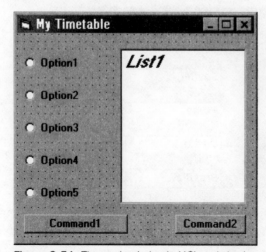

Figure 2.34 The project's basic HCI and the improved version

Writing the program

Plan for the *ShowSubjects* procedure

From the **Tools** menu create a procedure to fill the list box with the required subjects. The procedure will:

- if the Monday option is selected, clear the list box and display subjects for Monday
- if the Tuesday option is selected, clear the list box and display subjects for Tuesday
- if the Wednesday option is selected, clear the list box and display subjects for Wednesday
- if the Thursday option is selected, clear the list box and display subjects for Thursday
- if the Friday option is selected, clear the list box and display subjects for Friday.

Code for the *ShowSubjects* procedure

Remember to create a procedure from the **Tools** menu! Also, have your weekly subjects timetable ready so that you can replace *Subject* in the code below with the real names. The code will be:

```
Sub ShowSubjects()
LstSubjects.Clear
If Option1.Value = True Then
    LstSubjects.AddItem "French"
    LstSubjects.AddItem "English"
    LstSubjects.AddItem "Maths"
    LstSubjects.AddItem "Computing"
    LstSubjects.AddItem "PE"
    LstSubjects.AddItem "History"
    LstSubjects.AddItem "Biology"
End If

If Option2.Value = True Then
    LstSubjects.AddItem "Subject"
    LstSubjects.AddItem "Subject"
    LstSubjects.AddItem "Subject"
    LstSubjects.AddItem "Subject"
    LstSubjects.AddItem "Subject"
    LstSubjects.AddItem "Subject"
    LstSubjects.AddItem "Subject"
End If

If Option3.Value = True Then
    LstSubjects.AddItem "Subject"
    LstSubjects.AddItem "Subject"
    LstSubjects.AddItem "Subject"
    LstSubjects.AddItem "Subject"
    LstSubjects.AddItem "Subject"
    LstSubjects.AddItem "Subject"
    LstSubjects.AddItem "Subject"
End If
```

```
If Option4.Value = True Then
    LstSubjects.AddItem "Subject"
    LstSubjects.AddItem "Subject"
    LstSubjects.AddItem "Subject"
    LstSubjects.AddItem "Subject"
    LstSubjects.AddItem "Subject"
    LstSubjects.AddItem "Subject"
    LstSubjects.AddItem "Subject"
End If

If Option5.Value = True Then
    LstSubjects.AddItem "Subject"
    LstSubjects.AddItem "Subject"
    LstSubjects.AddItem "Subject"
    LstSubjects.AddItem "Subject"
    LstSubjects.AddItem "Subject"
    LstSubjects.AddItem "Subject"
    LstSubjects.AddItem "Subject"
End If
End Sub
```

Remember that, even though you have changed the captions of the option buttons to Monday … Friday, *Visual Basic still knows them only as Option1, Option2, Option3, Option4 and Option5.*

If an option button's value is **True** it means that the user has selected that option button. All the other option buttons are therefore set to **False** – that is, not selected.

Figure 2.35 shows the expected result when the option button for Monday is clicked (set to **True**).

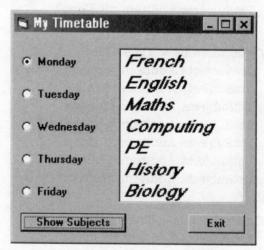

Figure 2.35 The result of clicking the Monday option

Now you try

Create a pop quiz program that asks the user to make a choice out of four options. The question to be asked is: 'What singer performs ... (name of a song)?'

If that works, change the project to do a quiz of your choice. Look at Figure 2.36 for an example of a form for a football quiz.

> This label should dispay either 'Correct' or 'Wrong!' when the user clicks the button.

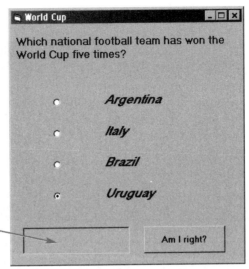

Figure 2.36 A football quiz program running

 Now you try

Try to recreate the calculator program of Chapter 1.11, but this time use what you have learned in this unit. Use the **OptionButton** control and give the user the choices of addition, subtraction, multiplication and division. Look at Figure 2.37 for some ideas.

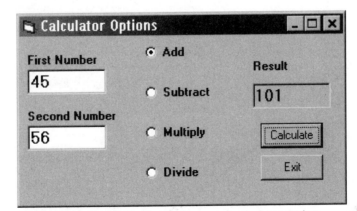

Figure 2.37 Suggestion for the improved calculator project

You may find this hint useful for your coding:

```
FirstNumber = Val(Text1.Text)
SecondNumber = Val(Text2.Text)
```

The rest is over to you!

Now you try

Fantasyland Parks is a popular theme park organisation that sells tickets for adults and children. Extra is charged if you want to go on the white-water rapids trip.

The cost for the day is:

	Day	Day + rapids trip
Adult	£10.50	£15.00
Child	£5.70	£8.00

Write a program to calculate a trip for a group of 40 people. The following tickets are required:

	Day	Day + rapids trip
Adult	2	8
Child	20	10

Your program should display the group costs for:

- adults: day cost plus rapids trip cost
- children: day cost plus rapids trip cost
- total group cost for the trip.

UNIT 2 SUMMARY

What did you learn?

Picture this
(Adding graphics to a form)

- You can place a picture in a picture box on a form with the command:
  Picture1 = LoadPicture("*Path to a file*").
- You can set its **Autosize** property by using the Property window and setting its property to **True**.

Passwords
(Do ... Loop Until)

- A **Do ... Loop Until** loop tests a condition at the end of the loop so it will be entered at least once and if the condition is **False** the loop continues until the condition is set to **True**.
- You looked at a structure diagram to help you design your programs.

Finding maximum and minimum values
(Dim)

- To set aside room for a list in the computer's memory, you use Dim. For example:

      Dim Heights(20).

- You can use **MaxNo** and **MinNo** to find maximum and minimum values. For example:

      MaxNo Heights(), 10
      MinNo Heights(), 10.

- You can place a value into a label at runtime after user input from **InputBox**.

Sports day improved
(Nested loops with For ... Next)

Nested loops allow you to repeat a set of repeated actions. There is an *outer loop* and an *inner loop*.

The computer making decisions
(If ... Then)

- You saw how the computer can be asked to make decisions with the construct **If ... Then**.
- A **combo box** is similar to a list box except that you have to click its pull-down arrow to see its contents.
- You can type new entries into a combo box and can save room on your form.

Option buttons
(If Option1.Value = True Then)

You can use **option buttons** to give choices in your program. For example:

      If Option1.Value = True Then
          Do something
          Do something else
      End If

3.1 If ... Then ... Else ... End If

The computer making decisions

You have learned how to use **If ... Then** to get the program to make decisions. When we use **If ... Then** we have to repeat the **If ... Then** statement in order to get the computer to carry out a different action if the former condition was not true. In this chapter you will learn to use the **If ... Then ... Else ... End If** construction which will allow you to avoid having to repeat **If ... Then**.

So for example, our **Geography** program had to test a combo box for a correct or wrong entry:

```
If Combo1.Text = "Paris" Then MsgBox "Correct"
If Combo1.Text <> "Paris" Then MsgBox "Wrong"
```

With **If ... Then ... Else ... End If** we could ask the computer to carry out the same actions in a more grammatically elegant way:

```
If Combo1.Text = "Paris" Then
    MsgBox "Correct"
Else
    MsgBox "Wrong"
End If
```

You will agree that the second form, using **Else**, makes more sense grammatically.

Later in this chapter you will be using **If ... Then ... Else ... End If** to create a quiz about rivers. You will create a project where the user will be asked some general knowledge questions. The computer will notify the user if the answer is correct and give the right answers after the last question has been answered at the end of the program.

How to use If ... Then ... Else ... End If

To practise the principles, first let's use the program you saved earlier as **Geography** and modify it by using the **If ... Then ... Else ... End If** construction. The program, however, will perform in the same way. First open the **Geography** program and make the form visible, as in Figure 3.1.

Figure 3.1 The old form for the Geography project

Double-click the button to open its code window, seen in the top part of Figure 3.2. You are going to replace the code in this button with what you see in the bottom part of the figure.

First delete the Visual Basic coding that is between the lines **Private Sub cmdAmIRight** and **End Sub**. Then type in the new code, which is:

```
If Combo1.Text = "Paris" Then
    MsgBox "Correct"
Else
    MsgBox "Wrong"
End If
```

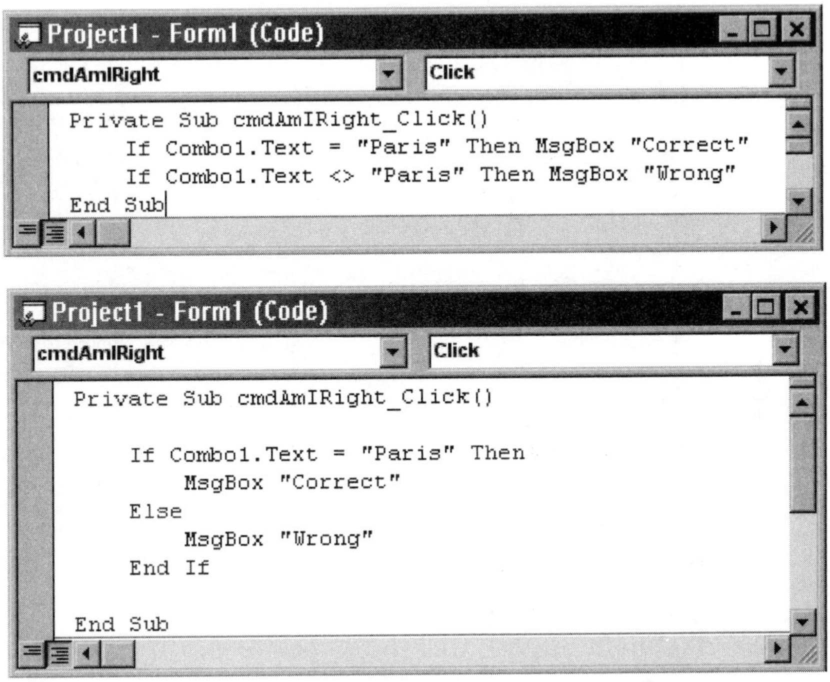

Figure 3.2 Replacing the old code

Run the program

Press **F5** to run the program. If you get the messages 'Correct' and 'Wrong' as you did for the first version of the program, then you will know that the changes you have made have been successful. If your program comes up with an error, it is most likely that a Visual Basic instruction has been mistyped. If your program stops with an error, select **End** from the **Run** menu and search for your mistake.

You have just learned to use the **If ... Then ... Else ... End If** construction to simplify **If ... Then** and give the Visual Basic coding a more natural flow to the logic.

Creating the human–computer interface (HCI)

We now turn to the *rivers quiz project* mentioned earlier. We will first design the HCI interface for the quiz program, and then plan the instructions for the procedures to ask the questions and display the answers.

Plan for the form

Create two list boxes, one for the countries and one for the rivers (**lstShowCountries** and **lstAnswers**). Set the list boxes' **Visible** property to **False**.

Next use the **List** property of the list boxes to enter the data (countries and rivers). Here are the steps:

1 Click the **lstShowCountries** list box to select it.

2 Press **F4** to bring up its Properties window.

3 Select its **List** property and click the pull-down list to allow you to type the list of countries, as in the first part of Figure 3.3. As you type the list you will need to do **Ctrl + Enter** to start new lines (if you just press **Enter** the list will disappear!).

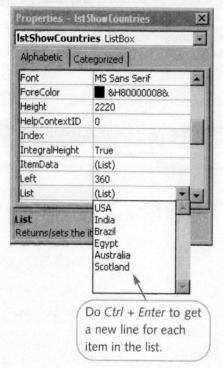
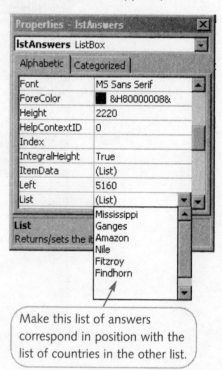

Do *Ctrl + Enter* to get a new line for each item in the list.

Make this list of answers correspond in position with the list of countries in the other list.

Figure 3.3 Using the **List** property to enter your data

4 Do the same for the **lstAnswers** list box to add the list of answers to its **List** property, as in the second part of Figure 3.3. The list of answers *must* correspond in position in the list with the list of countries in the other list.

You have now entered the data. The remaining steps are as follows, using the techniques you have already learned:

- Set the form's caption to **Rivers Quiz**.
- Create a label for the form above the list boxes and set its caption to **Countries and Rivers Quiz**.
- Create a command button to start the quiz. Set its name property to **cmdStartQuiz** and its caption to **Start Quiz**.
- Create a command button to end the program. Set its name property to **cmdExit** and its caption to **Exit**.
- Set the font size and style for the list boxes to bold 14pt.

Figure 3.4 shows the form after it has been designed.

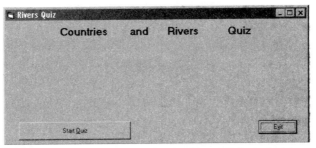

Figure 3.4 The form design for the Rivers Quiz project

Writing the program

The program will loop five times, asking a different question each time. The user will input the answer with **InputBox**. The message 'Correct' or 'Wrong' will be displayed depending on the user's answer. After the five questions have been asked the program will display the countries and the corresponding rivers in the two list boxes.

Plan for the *cmdStartQuiz* button

1 Loop for five times.

2 Ask the user for a river with InputBox.

3 If the user's answer matches with the correct country, then ...

4 ... put up a message 'Correct' with MsgBox.

5 Else ...

6 ... put up a message 'Wrong' with MsgBox.

7 End the **If** test.

8 End the loop.

9 Set the countries list box to visible.

10 Set the answers list box to visible.

Code for the *Start Quiz* button

The required code is:

```
For Quiz = 1 To 5
MyAnswer = InputBox("In which country does the " &
                            lstAnswers.List(Quiz) & " river flow?")
If MyAnswer = lstShowCountries.List(Quiz) Then
    MsgBox "Correct"
Else
    MsgBox "Wrong"
End If
Next Quiz
lstShowCountries.Visible = True
lstAnswers.Visible = True
```

Double-click the **cmdStartQuiz** button to bring up its code window and type this code into its click event procedure, as in Figure 3.5.

```
Project1 - Form1 (Code)
cmdStartQuiz                                          Click

    Private Sub cmdStartQuiz_Click()
        For Quiz = 1 To 5
            MyAnswer = InputBox("In which country does the " & lstAnswers.List(Quiz) & " river flow?")
            If MyAnswer = lstShowCountries.List(Quiz) Then
                MsgBox "Correct"
            Else
                MsgBox "Wrong"
            End If
        Next Quiz
        lstShowCountries.Visible = True
        lstAnswers.Visible = True
    End Sub
```

Figure 3.5 The code window for the **cmdStartQuiz** button click event

Code for the *Exit* button

As you have seen many times before, the code for the **Exit** button is simply

> End

Type that command in the button's click event window.

Running and testing the program

When you start to run the program the two list boxes should *not* be visible (as in Figure 3.4). If you find that the list boxes are visible then stop the program and set their **Visible** property to **false**.

Click the **Start Quiz** button and the program asks a question, as in the first part of Figure 3.6. The message 'Correct' or 'Wrong' appears depending on the user's input.

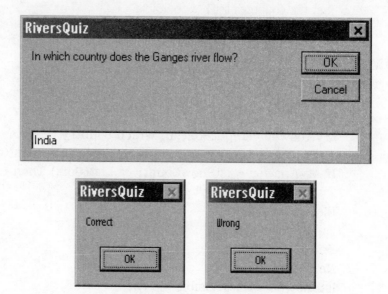

Figure 3.6 The program running, and the two possible results

After the questions have been asked the two list boxes are made visible to reveal the countries and the answers, as in Figure 3.7.

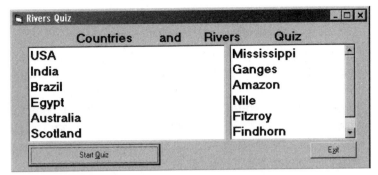

Figure 3.7 At the end the program displays the answers

 Now you try

1 Create a program to test the user's knowledge of music groups and their songs. Make the computer ask between ten and twenty questions and give a suitable response depending on whether the answers are right or wrong – for example, 'Well done!' or 'No, that's not right'.

2 Create a program that tests a password typed into a text box control. Use **If … Then … Else** to allow the computer to put up messages like 'OK, you have access!' or 'No, that's not the password. You do not have access.'

Hint: When a computer program asks for a password it is sensible to mask the real characters of the password typed, by using another character – usually an asterisk (*). To do this in your program, select the text box control, press **F4**, and type in an asterisk (*) into its **Password** property.

3.2 How to use parameters

Finding the area of a rectangle

It is good programming practice to create programs that use procedures to carry out specific tasks. Earlier you learned how to create a procedure, and then you used procedures that were specially written for you to find the minimum and maximum of a set of numbers. These were stored in a module for future use if required. Procedures that are intended to be reusable often require **parameters**. Parameters are variable placeholders that can move values around in a program in and out of procedures or functions.

Take a look back at Chapter 2.3 and note that in the **GetHeights** procedure that you created you made use of another two procedures **MinNo** and **MaxNo** that worked out minimum and maximum values from a list of numbers. All you had to do to use them was to pass a couple of parameters into them. Below are the two lines of code that called the two procedures and passed the parameters into them:

```
MaxNo Heights(), 10
MinNo Heights(), 10
```

Heights() and 10 in each line are the parameters – the list of numbers and the number of values in the list, respectively.

In this chapter we will look more closely at how parameters are passed back and forth in and out of procedures.

Let us imagine that we want a program to calculate the area of a rectangle. We can create a procedure to do that. Let's call our procedure **CalculateArea**. To be able to do its job the procedure will need to receive from the program the parameters *Length* and *Breadth*. The procedure, once it has done its job, will need to send the program the answer of the calculation it has carried out with *Length* and *Breadth*, so it requires another parameter, *Area*, to send the answer back to the program. Diagrammatically it looks like Figure 3.8.

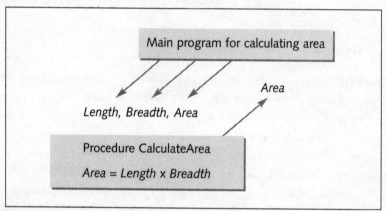

Figure 3.8 The procedure receives three parameters and sends back one

Note that *Length* and *Breadth* are passed with their values already ascertained so they are not required to be passed back to the main program. In other words the procedure will just use the values that *Length* and *Breadth* already contain and the procedure will not change their values. This is called **passing by value**. In Visual Basic we tell the procedure that *Length* and *Breadth* are being passed by value by using the keyword **ByVal**.

The parameter *Area* has to be passed back to the main program. The procedure will calculate the area and place the result into the *Area* parameter. This is called **passing by reference**. This is the default in Visual Basic, so we do not have to inform the procedure. When we create the procedure the formal parameters are defined as follows:

```
Sub CalculateArea(ByVal Length, ByVal Breadth, Area)
    Area = Length * Breadth
End Sub
```

When you create the procedure and the formal parameters it is important to separate the parameters with commas. The names do not have to be the same as in the main program, so in the example above *LengthIn*, *BreadthIn* and *AreaOut* would work.

When we want to use the procedure in the main program we have to **call** it. In calling the procedure we use the *actual parameters*, like this:

```
CalculateArea Length, Breadth, Area
```

Note that the formal parameters must match the **actual** parameters both in number and in position in the list passed. Also note that the list of parameters is separated with commas.

Visual Basic requires that **actual** parameters be declared before they can be used. **Declaring** means that you tell Visual Basic what parameters you are going to use with the keyword **Dim**:

```
Dim Length, Breadth, Area
```

You would place this declaration in the declarations section of the program, as in Figure 3.9.

```
Area - Form1 (Code)                                    _ □ ×
(General)                    ▼   (Declarations)                ▼

    Dim Length, Breadth, Area

    Sub CalculateArea(ByVal Length, ByVal Breadth, Area)
    Area = Length * Breadth
    End Sub

    Sub DisplayResults(ByVal Length, ByVal Breadth, Area)
    Label1.Caption = Length
    Label2.Caption = Breadth
    Label3.Caption = Area
    End Sub
```

Figure 3.9 The declaration can be seen at the top of this code window

Notice that the declarations section comes in the general area of the code window. You will be given step-by-step instructions when you implement the code later in the chapter.

That is the theory of parameter passing. We will now create our **Area** program to put all this into practice.

Creating the human–computer interface (HCI)

We will use labels to display the length and breadth entered by the user, and a label will also display the area calculated. A button will call three procedures – **GetDimensions**, **CalculateArea** and **DisplayResults**.

Plan for the form

1 Create three labels for the length, breadth and area.
Set their **BorderStyle** property to 1 – Fixed Single.

2 Create three labels and set their captions to document the display.

3 Create a button and set its caption to **Find Area** and its name property to **cmdFindArea**. It will call the three procedures **GetDimensions**, **CalculateArea**, and **DisplayResults**.

4 Set the form's caption to **Area**.

5 Set the size of fonts to match what you see here on the form in Figure 3.10.

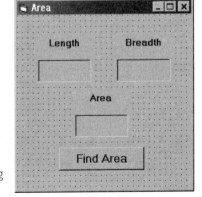

Figure 3.10 The form containing six labels and one button

Writing the program

Plan for the procedure *GetDimensions*

1 Use InputBox to get the *Length*.

2 Use InputBox to get the *Breadth*.

Plan for the procedure *CalculateArea*

Set *Area* to be *Length* times *Breadth*.

Plan for the procedure *DisplayResults*

1 Set **Label1** to *Length*.

2 Set **Label2** to *Breadth*.

3 Set **Label3** to *Area*.

Declaring the parameters *Length, Breadth* and *Area*

To declare the variable parameters you must place them in the declarations section of the code window. Follow these steps to declare the parameters.

1 Double-click the form to open a code window.

2 Pull down the menu list (as on the left of Figure 3.11) and select General from the list.

3 Type this line into the declarations section (as on the right of Figure 3.11):

```
Dim Length, Breadth, Area
```

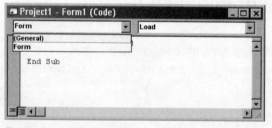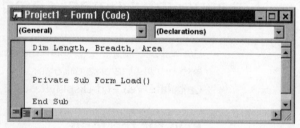

Figure 3.11 Making the required declarations in a code window

Code for *cmdFindArea*

The required code is:

```
GetDimensions Length, Breadth
CalculateArea Length, Breadth, Area
DisplayResults Length, Breadth, Area
```

Double-click the **cmdFindArea** button to get its code window and type this code into its click event procedure, as in Figure 3.12.

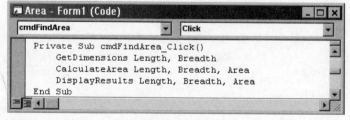

Figure 3.12 The code for **cmdFindArea** has been entered

Code for the procedure *GetDimensions*

With a code window open, create a procedure using the **Tools** menu – see Figure 3.13.

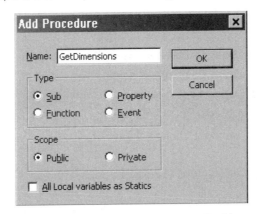

Figure 3.13 How to create the procedure GetDimensions

In the code window you have opened you need to type in the parameters *Length* and *Breadth* into the formal parameters brackets. The parameters *Length* and *Breadth* are **passed by reference** because we want the procedure to supply values into them. The code is:

```
Sub GetDimensions(Length, Breadth)
    Length = InputBox("Please enter the length.")
    Breadth = InputBox("Please enter the breadth.")
End Sub
```

The code window should look like Figure 3.14 when you have typed in the procedure.

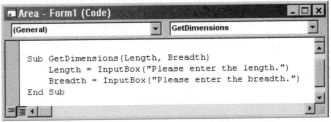

Figure 3.14 The code for the procedure GetDimensions has been entered

Code for the procedure *CalculateArea*

Create another procedure from the **Tools** menu for **CalculateArea**, just as you did above. Here is the code:

```
Sub CalculateArea(ByVal Length, ByVal Breadth, Area)
    Area = Length * Breadth
End Sub
```

Note that you must include the formal parameters in the brackets *at the start of the procedure*. Also note that the parameters *Length* and *Breadth* are passed, in this case, by **value** (**ByVal**) as their values are not to be changed. The parameter *Area* is passed by **reference** because its value will be updated by the procedure's calculation and passed back into the program.

Code for the procedure *DisplayResults*

Create the procedure **DisplayResults** and type this code into it:

```
Sub DisplayResults(ByVal Length, ByVal Breadth, ByVal Area)
    Label1.Caption = Length
    Label2.Caption = Breadth
    Label3.Caption = Area
End Sub
```

All the parameters are passed by **value** this time because this procedure will only display the values and not change them in any way.

Running and testing the program

When you have finished typing in your program, test it and see that it is giving the correct results. Click the **Find Area** button several times and input different values.

When the program is working correctly the form should show the values entered and the calculated area. An example is shown in Figure 3.15. Save your project as **Area**.

Figure 3.15 An example of the program running

Jargon buster

ByVal – We use ByVal in front of a formal parameter to tell Visual Basic that we don't want the value of the parameter changed nor passed back to the program. What Visual Basic does, in fact, is send only a *copy* of the variable to the procedure and the copy can be destroyed when the procedure finishes.

ByRef – You can, if you want, put ByRef in front of a formal parameter when you are passing by reference. However, as was said earlier, Visual Basic treats any parameter as being passed by reference *unless* ByVal is used. Both these formal declarations are correct:

```
Sub CalculateArea(ByVal Length, ByVal Breadth, Area)
    Area = Length * Breadth
End Sub
```
and
```
Sub CalculateArea(ByVal Length, ByVal Breadth, ByRef Area)
    Area = Length * Breadth
End Sub
```

Learning to use Visual Basic

Now you try

Assume that the price of carpeting a room is £5.70 a square metre. Use the program you have just completed to find the price of carpeting for the dimensions input by the user. You will need to create an extra new procedure to work out the price for the area calculated.

- What new parameter will have to be declared and passed to the procedure?
- What parameters will the procedure require?
- Will the parameters be passed by value or by reference?
- How are you going to get the price per square metre?
- Will you use another InputBox?

Plan what you are going to do. First redesign the HCI – that should get you started!

Supertask

Now you try

With the knowledge you have learned about parameter passing, design a project to work out the *area of a circle*.

The formula for the area of a circle is π (pi) times the radius squared, or π x r x r. Set the value of π to 3.14.

Ask the user to provide a value for the radius. Create a procedure called **CircleArea** and decide what parameters you will pass to it. Which will be passed by value and which by reference? Declare the variables you will require in the declarations section of your code.

3.3 Using arrays (1)

You have learnt how to use **Dim** to let Visual Basic know how many numbers a list will hold. You then could pass the list as a parameter to the procedures **MinNo** and **MaxNo**. The Visual Basic name for this type of list is an **array**.

What exactly is an array? An array is a special type of *variable*. An array allows us to group a list of similar data under one variable name. We can then refer to each item in the array by using the name and a subscript or index. For example, here are two arrays, one holding names and another holding numbers:

Names()	Ages()
"John"	75
"Mary"	22
"Sally"	16
"Paul"	48

The first array has the variable name **Names()** and the second array's variable name is **Ages()**. The brackets after each of the variables are necessary to tell Visual Basic that we are referring to arrays.

In code we can refer to a particular item in the array by putting a number into the brackets, like this: **Names(4)**. The number in the brackets is the **index** or subscript that pinpoints one of the pieces of data in the array.

The program gives each of the items in the array an index number, so we can regard the arrays as being stored in the computer's memory like this:

Names(1) = "John"	Ages(1) = 75
Names(2) = "Mary"	Ages(2) = 22
Names(3) = "Sally"	Ages(3) = 16
Names(4) = "Paul"	Ages(4) = 48

Arrays can be different sizes. One might have four items like above; another array may have room for 30 items. We tell the program how many we want in the **Dim** statement, like this: **Dim Names(4)** and **Dim Ages(4)**.

Arrays are useful because they help you track large amounts of data in ways that would be impractical using traditional variables. It is easier to manipulate an array of data in a loop using its indexes rather than different variables. Think of it this way: to take 30 people to Aberdeen you would arrange to send them all in one bus, and not 30 buses with one person in each! Think of a bus as a variable and the bus that takes them to Aberdeen as an array of people called Bus().

Perhaps you are wondering why we need to bother with arrays when we already have the **List** object. List boxes have their existence on a form for display purposes. We might, however, require their contents in another part of the program. We need to use arrays as parameters to send information to procedures. This we cannot do with lists. However, we can transfer the contents of a list box into an array and then use the array as a parameter into a procedure.

Filling an array

Filling an element in an array with data involves knowing the name of the array and the number of the index where you want the data placed. So let us say that we have declared an array to hold the names of our favourite team with a **Dim** statement like this:

```
Dim SquadNames(11)
```

You now have 11 locations in the **SquadNames()** array where you can place data. (Actually you have 12 locations because Visual Basic creates a location 0, but we won't worry about that just now.)

A Visual Basic instruction to place a name in location 7 could look like this:

```
SquadNames(7) = "Ronaldo"
```

Location 7 of the **SquadNames()** array would continue to hold the data "Ronaldo" until updated by Visual Basic code. If you required to display the data of this location in a label on the form for the project, you could use the instruction:

```
Label1.Caption = SquadNames(7)
```

To get the full team into the array using this method would require the following statements:

```
SquadNames(1) = "Marcos"
SquadNames(2) = "Cafu"
SquadNames(3) = "Roberto Carlos"
SquadNames(4) = "Kleberson"
SquadNames(5) = "Gilberto Silva"
SquadNames(6) = "Lucio"
SquadNames(7) = "Ronaldo"
SquadNames(8) = "Rivaldo"
SquadNames(9) = "Ronaldinho"
SquadNames(10) = "Roque Junior"
SquadNames(11) = "Denilson"
```

A very useful aspect of the array structure is that the index can itself be a variable which allows us to use the control variable in a loop to quickly pick out a data item. For example, study this fragment of code that displays in a label the location a name appears in:

```
PlayerName = Inputbox("Please enter the name of the player.")
For Player = 1 To 11
    If PlayerName = SquadName(Player) Then Label1.Caption = Player
Next Player
```

The control variable **Player** is used to pinpoint the index of the array where the name is located.

We will create a simple project to get our list of names into an array and then display any name from the list in a label. The user will be prompted for an index number and the program will display the corresponding name in the list.

Creating the human–computer interface (HCI)

1 Create four labels with font style bold size 12pt. Label1's caption is '**Player**', Label2 will display the name of the player, Label3's caption is '**has index**', and Label4 will hold the index input by the user.

2 Create a button and set its caption to '**Enter index**' with font style bold and size 12pt. Set its name to **cmdEnterIndex**.

The form when you have finished designing it should look like the left part of Figure 3.16. Note that the captions for labels 2 and 4 have been deleted and their **BorderStyle** property is set to 1 – Fixed Single for that sunken look.

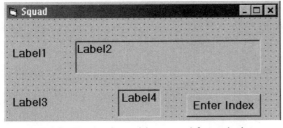 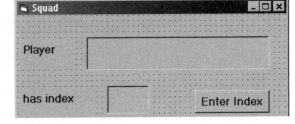

Figure 3.16 The basic and improved form designs

Writing the program

All the coding for the program will be in the **cmdEnterIndex** button.

Plan for the *cmdEnterIndex* button

1 Declare the array to hold the names.

2 Set the array to 11 names of players.

3 Get the index from the user.

4 Display the player's name with the input index in Label2.

5 Display the index input in Label4.

Code for the *cmdEnterIndex* button

The required code is:

```
Dim SquadNames(11)

SquadNames(1) = "Marcos"
SquadNames(2) = "Cafu"
SquadNames(3) = "Roberto Carlos"
SquadNames(4) = "Kleberson"
SquadNames(5) = "Gilberto Silva"
SquadNames(6) = "Lucio"
SquadNames(7) = "Ronaldo"
SquadNames(8) = "Rivaldo"
SquadNames(9) = "Ronaldinho"
SquadNames(10) = "Roque Junior"
SquadNames(11) = "Denilson"

IndexNumber = InputBox("Please enter an index number.")
Label2.Caption = SquadNames(IndexNumber)
Label4.Caption = IndexNumber
```

Double-click the **cmdEnterIndex** button and type the code into its click event procedure.

Running and testing the program

When the program runs the user clicks the button and is asked to input an index number. The program then displays both the name of the player with that index in the array of names and the index itself, as in Figure 3.17. Try all the indices from 1 to 11 and see that the correct names are displayed.

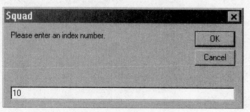

Figure 3.17 The program running

Learning to use Visual Basic

If you try an index greater than 11, Visual Basic will come up with an error, as in Figure 3.18 (remember that *subscript* is another name for the index). As the error says, the subscript for the array is out of range. Visual Basic is telling you something you already know, that the array **SquadNames()** was declared only for 0 to 11 items of data. Do not worry about this. The program requires an error trap that we are not covering at this stage.

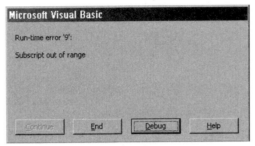

Figure 3.18 Visual Basic reports an error if the index is out of range

Click the **End** button and run the program again. Then save your project as **Squad**.

Jargon buster

Debug – When a program is suspended with an error a window appears with options for you to end the program or to debug. If you choose to debug, the code window will be displayed, with the error highlighted. If you correct the error, you can either press **F5** to continue running the program or you can end the program by choosing **End** from the **Run** menu.

On some occasions the corrections that you make in debug mode are such that Visual Basic cannot continue. Visual Basic, in this case, displays a warning message. If you click **OK**, Visual Basic will make the changes and the program will end. You will have to restart the program if you want to continue and run the changes. Figure 3.19 shows the warning message box that appears.

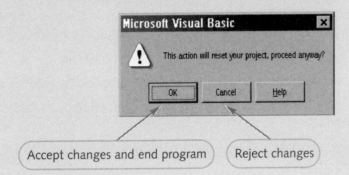

Figure 3.19 Visual Basic gives you the option to accept or reject its changes to the program code when there is an error

Now you try

Design a project that uses an array to hold the names of songs. Arrange it so that the index represents the position of the song in the charts. Your program should allow the user to input an index and the program will display on the form the name of the song and confirm its position in the charts.

Using lists with arrays

As you have seen, in Visual Basic projects list boxes constitute an important aspect of the language in displaying information on forms. It is also important to be able to manipulate these lists within the code of the program and pass their data content as parameters to procedures. For this purpose we need to use arrays in combination with list boxes.

Let's remind ourselves how the **AddItem** method is used to store data in a list:

```
List1.AddItem "You're Breaking my Heart"
List2.AddItem "10"
```

We had to store the information in the lists before we ran the program.

Now we will take a look at a more flexible method of storing data. We can use arrays to carry out more complex tasks like sorting and searching the lists.

In this chapter you will create a program to store names of cars in an array, pass the array as a parameter to a procedure for sorting, and display the contents of the array in a list box.

Creating the human–computer interface (HCI)

On your CD-ROM for this book you will find the project **Cars**. You must open this project as it contains the **sort** procedure you will require and the form to start you off.

Plan for the cars form

1 Create a list box and set its name property to **ListCars**.

2 Create a text box and set its name property to **TextCars** (for input of cars).

3 Create a command button and set its caption property to **Add Cars** and its name to **cmdAddCars**.

4 Create a command button and set its caption property to **Sort Cars** and its name to **cmdSortCars**.

5 Create a command button and set its caption property to **Exit** and its name to **cmdExit**.

6 Create user-friendly labels on the form to explain what is going on.

Pay close attention to the naming of objects on the form as these names will be used in the program code. Your program will fail if the names you give them do not match the names used in the coding.

Your form should look something like Figure 3.20 when you have designed it.

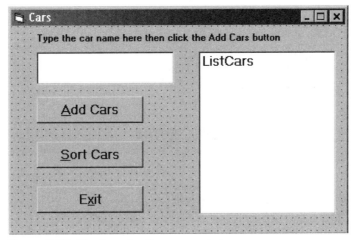

Figure 3.20 The form for the cars project

Writing the program

The two main buttons on the form are **cmdAddCars** and **cmdSortCars**. The **cmdAddCars** button will move the input that the user types into the text box **TextCars** and add it to the list box **ListCars**. The **cmdSortCars** button will call a procedure **SortCars** that you will create.

Plan for the *cmdAddCars* button

1 Set the **ListCars** list box to the input in the text box.

2 Clear the text box **TextCars**.

3 Place the cursor in the text box ready for the user.

Code for the *cmdAddCars* button

The required code is:

```
Sub cmdAddCars_Click()
    ListCars.AddItem TextCars
    TextCars = " "
    TextCars.SetFocus
End Sub
```

Plan for the *cmdSortCars* button

Call the procedure **SortCars**.

Code for the *cmdSortCars* button

The required code is:

```
Sub cmdSortCars_Click()
    SortCars
End Sub
```

Plan for the *SortCars* procedure

1 Declare the **Cars()** array to hold five items.

2 Loop for five times.

3 Set the array element to the **ListCars** item.

4 End the for loop.

5 Call the procedure **OrderWords**.

6 Clear the **ListCars** list box.

7 Loop for five times.

8 Set the **ListCars** item to the array element.

9 End the for loop.

Code for the *SortCars* procedure

You need to create a procedure called **SortCars**. Double-click the form and from the **Tools** menu select **Add Procedure**. The code to enter is:

```
Sub SortCars()
    Dim Cars(5)
    'First loop
    For make = 1 To 5
        Cars(make) = ListCars.List(make - 1)
    Next make
    OrderWords Cars(), 5
    ListCars.Clear
    'Second loop
    For make = 1 To 5
    ListCars.AddItem Cars(make)
    Next make
End Sub
```

The first loop (note the comment line) fills the array **Cars()** with the contents of the list box **ListCars**. This is necessary as we require to pass the array to the **OrderWords** procedure. We can't use the list box as a parameter. The second loop redisplays the cars in their sorted form in the list box.

Note that the **OrderWords** procedure needs two parameters to be passed to it: the array and the number of items in the array.

Running and testing the program

The program runs and waits for the user to type a name of a car into the text box. The name is added to the list box when the **Add Cars** button is clicked. Click the **Add Cars** button five times to add names into the list box. When you have five names of cars in the list box click the **Sort Cars** button. The names should then reappear sorted in the list box.

Save the project to update the changes you have made.

Now you try

For this task, open the project called **SortLowHigh** which you will find in a folder called **OrderNumbersLowHigh** on your CD-ROM.

There is a new procedure called **OrderNumbers** which will sort numbers. It requires three parameters like this:

- **OrderNumbers Nums(), 10, "High"** if you want to sort from high to low (descending)
- **OrderNumbers Nums(), 10 , "Low"** if you want to sort from low to high (ascending)

(the quotes are obligatory around Low and High).

Use this procedure to write a project that accepts a list of ten numbers and displays the numbers sorted either high-to-low or low-to-high as the user requests by clicking appropriate buttons (see Figure 3.21).

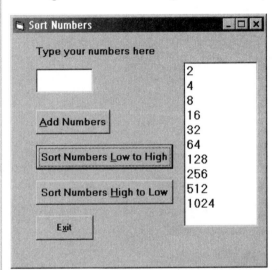
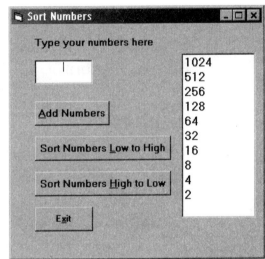

Figure 3.21 An example of what you are aiming to produce as a project

Hint: When you put the ListNumbers into the array, make your line this:

```
Numbers(index) = Val(ListNumbers.List(index -1))
```

The **Val** is required to make the values compatible with the numeric array.

3.5 Connecting lists

A diary

You have seen how useful lists can be in Visual Basic for displaying information. However, a problem with creating lists on a form is that they do not relate to each other. For example, say that you created two lists on a form, one to display a list of names of people and the other to display their corresponding ages. You then decide to put the names in alphabetical order, so you set the first list's **sorted** property to **true** and run the program. You will find that now the lists do not match up with the names to the ages as you had planned.

The programming that is required in Visual Basic to make the lists correspond to each other using arrays is quite complex at this stage of your programming course, so you will find some pre-prepared library procedures on the CD-ROM that will help you get the job done. You will still have to plan the arrays that you will use for the various lists and how they are passed as parameters to the procedures.

We will create a program that uses two lists. One will hold names and the other will hold telephone numbers. We will also sort the lists of names into alphabetical order. We can do this because we will use the pre-prepared procedures that will connect the lists to create connected lists.

Creating the human–computer interface (HCI)

Before you begin to design this project you need to open a project called **Diary** on your CD-ROM. Use the form *Diary* in the project to create the following objects.

Plan for the form

The form requires two list boxes, two labels and two buttons (see Figure 3.22). The procedures we are going to use require the two list box objects, otherwise the program will not work.

1 Create two lists, **List1** and **List2** (do not rename these list boxes).

2 Create two labels with captions **Names** and **Numbers**.

3 Create a command button **Get Names and Numbers**.

4 Create another command button **Exit** to end the program.

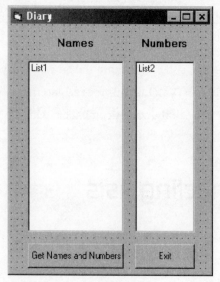

Figure 3.22 The diary form

Writing the program

With the computer it is easy to store lists of names and numbers. You can use a pre-prepared procedure to ask for pairs of names and numbers and it does not matter in what order you type the pairs, the computer will sort them and display them using other procedures. We will plan a program to take in pairs of names and telephone numbers and get the computer to sort them and display the sorted lists.

Plan for the *Diary* procedure

1 Allocate space for the list of names.

2 Allocate space for the list of numbers.

3 Put the names and numbers into the lists using the library procedure **TakeInWordsAndNumbers**.

4 Sort both lists, in order of names, using the procedure **OrderWordsAndNumbers**.

5 Display the lists using the procedure **DisplayNamesAndNumbers**.

Code for the *Diary* procedure

Create a procedure called **Diary** and type this code into it:

```
Dim Names(20)
Dim TelNums(20)
TakeInWordsAndNumbers Names(), TelNums(), 5
OrderWordsAndNumbers Names(), TelNums(), 5
DisplayNamesAndNumbers Names(), TelNums(), 5
```

The two arrays **Names()** and **TelNums()** will hold names and telephone numbers. Each of the library procedures takes three parameters: the two arrays and the number of items to be used.

The names of the procedures can also be written in a shortened form as they are rather long to type in:

- TakeInWordsAndNumbers can be shortened to **TIWAN**.
- OrderWordsAndNumbers can be shortened to **OWAN**.
- DisplayNamesAndNumbers can be shortened to **DNAN**.

The procedure **Diary** with the shortened names for the library procedures looks like this:

```
Dim Names(20)
Dim TelNums(20)
TIWAN Names(), TelNums(), 5
OWAN Names(), TelNums(), 5
DNAN Names(), TelNums(), 5
```

Plan and code for the *Get Names and Numbers* button

The plan is to call the procedure **Diary**. The code is simply

```
Diary
```

Code for the *Exit* button

As before, the code for the **Exit** button is simply

```
End
```

Running and testing the program

Before you run the program, prepare a list of five names and numbers. Now, without using the computer, put the names into alphabetical order. Run the program and type the names into the computer. Compare your ordered list with the computer's. Do you agree with the computer? If not, who's gone wrong?

The program asks for a word and then a number, as in Figure 3.23. **TakeInWordsAndNumbers** asks for five pairs of words and numbers. You type in five names and five numbers. The computer orders them into two lists, called **Names** and **TelNums**.

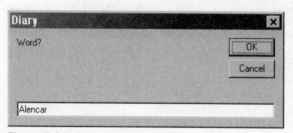 

Figure 3.23 The program asks for five names and five numbers

While the computer is sorting the lists with **OrderWordsAndNumbers** you won't see anything happening on the form, but the procedure **DisplayNamesAndNumbers** displays the two lists side by side, as in Figure 3.24.

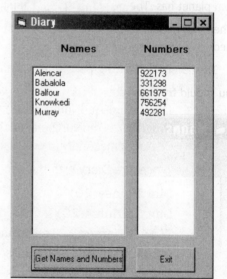

Figure 3.24 The names have been sorted into alphabetical order

When you are satisfied that your project is working correctly save it.

Now you try

Plan and write programs to solve these problems.

1 Alter the **Diary** program so that it will now deal with *ten* names and phone numbers.

2 Write down the names and heights of eight people in your class. Plan a program that will display lists of names and heights, in alphabetical order of their names.

Learning to use Visual Basic

Now you try

Open the project **Moons** that you will find on your CD-ROM.

Below is a table of our solar system's planets and the number of moons that each one has:

Planet	Number of moons
Mercury	0
Venus	0
Earth	1
Mars	2
Jupiter	16
Saturn	30
Uranus	15
Neptune	2
Pluto	1

There is a procedure **OrderNumbersAndWords** (**ONAW** for short) which will sort a list of numbers. Use it in a program using the above data about the planets to put into order the number of moons each planet has. The program should display the two lists side by side.

When you declare the array to hold the number of moons, set its type to **integer** as Visual Basic needs to do a numeric sort on this list. Declare it like this:

```
Dim NoOfMoons As Integer
```

You should try to produce a project that looks like the one in Figure 3.25.

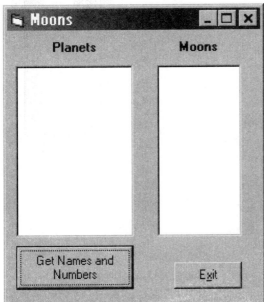

Figure 3.25 The **Moons** project running

3.6 Connected lists

Searching a diary

Although sorting a list is an important task that can be carried out, it could be argued that searching a list for information is even more important. Now that you have your **Diary** program working to store names and numbers, we will use it to store a list of five names and five numbers and then try to search either list for an individual item. The benefit of having both lists connected should become apparent.

A fundamental principle of searching connected lists is that you *use information that you know exists in one list to find information in the other list*. Below are two connected lists:

Name	Phone number
Stewart	135790
Ashford	246801
Murray	492281
Grandcoin	159371
Knwokedi	616014

Let's say that we wish to find the telephone number for Murray. We go down the first list until we come to Murray. That is in position 3, so we use this fact to find the telephone number. We count down 3 in the other list and that gives us 492281. This explains why the computer needs the name to find the number and the number to find the name.

When you dial 192 for Directory Enquiries you are asked for a name and a place name. With this information you are connected to a very powerful computer which searches its large database and finds the number in seconds anywhere in the country.

There are two procedures available to carry out searches. They are:

- **SearchForWord** (**SFW** for short)
- **SearchForNumber** (**SFN** for short).

In both cases you must pass three parameters with these procedures.

To display the results of your searches there are also two library procedures. They are:

- DisplayWordSearch(**DWS** for short)
- DisplayNumberSearch(**DNS** for short)

These two procedures take two parameters.

In this chapter you will create a program that will search for a telephone number if it is supplied with a name. We will use the same procedures to get the lists into the computer that we used with the **Diary** program. Then we will use the new search procedure to find the number.

Creating the human–computer interface (HCI)

Before you begin the design you need to open a project called **SearchDiary** on your CD-ROM. Use the form *SearchDiary* in the project to create the following objects.

Plan for form *SearchDiary*

1 Create two lists, **List1** and **List2** (do not rename these list boxes).

2 Create two labels with captions **Name requested** and **Number found**.

3 Create a command button **Get Details and Search**.

4 Create another command button **Exit** to quit.

The form should look like Figure 3.26.

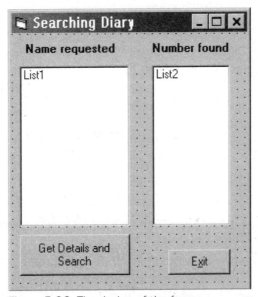

Figure 3.26 The design of the form

Writing the program

As you did for the **Diary** program, you will use the library procedure **TakeInWordsAndNumbers** to ask for pairs of names and numbers. The computer will search the list of names to find the name requested using the library procedure **SearchForWord** and use the position in the list where the name was found to locate the number in the numbers list. The program will then display them using another procedure **DisplayWordSearch**.

Plan for the procedure *SearchDiary*

1 Reserve space for two lists (five members long), names and numbers.

2 Get the lists into the computer.

3 Repeat.

4 Ask for a name.

5 Search for the name.

6 Display the search result ...

7 ... until the word 'Finished' is typed.

Code for the procedure *SearchDiary*

Create a procedure called **SearchDiary** and type this code into it:

```
Dim Names(20), Numbers(20)
TakeInWordsAndNumbers Names(), Numbers(), 5
Do
      Person = InputBox("Search for which name? Type Finished when done")
      SearchForWord Names(), Person, 5
      DisplayWordSearch Numbers(), Person
Loop Until Person = "Finished"
```

- The **Dim** statement reserves space for two lists of five names and numbers. **Dim Names(20), Numbers(20)** makes the computer reserve space for two lists: a list called **Names** holding up to 20 words, a list called **Numbers** holding up to 20 numbers.
- **TakeInWordsAndNumbers** then fills the lists with the names and telephone numbers you input.
- **Person = InputBox("Search for which name? Type Finished when done")** lets you put a name into the computer. From now on the variable **Person** in the program will hold whatever you typed in.

Once space has been reserved in the memory, the procedures listed below can be used.

- **TakeInWordsAndNumbers Names(), Numbers(), 5** was discussed before. It requires three parameters.
- **Person = InputBox("Search for which name? Type Finished when done")** lets us enter the name to be searched for into the computer.
- **SearchForWord Names(), Person, 5** passes the list of names, the name to be searched for and the length of the list to the procedure. The procedure will look down the list of five names until it comes to a name that matches the name you typed in for **Person** at the **InputBox** above. This will identify the position of the name and will be paired with the telephone number at the same position in the list of numbers.
- **DisplayWordSearch Numbers(), Person** will display the name searched for and also the phone number that is paired with it.
- The **Do ... Loop Until** construct allows us to get the computer to repeat a number of tasks until we type 'Finished'.

Plan and code for the *Get Details and Search* button

Call the procedure **SearchDiary**. The code is simply

```
SearchDiary
```

Code for the *Exit* button

As before, the code for the **Exit** button is simply

```
End
```

Running and testing the program

As you did in the previous chapter, before you run the program prepare a list of five names and numbers. The program will ask five times for a word and five times for a number which will put five items into each array. When the program asks for a name to search, enter one of the names you input. Check to see that the computer is giving you a number that corresponds with the name you input.

Save your project as **Search Diary**.

Now you try

The way the program works at present is that you have decided how many items will be entered into the arrays at design time. Change the program so that the user is prompted for the number of items that will be input.

Once you have the number from the user as a variable it can be used as the parameter that is passed to all the procedures that require it. So if the variable is **NoOfItems** it could be passed as a parameter like this:

```
TakeInWordsAndNumbers Names(), NoOfItems
```

3.7 Validating user input

The *IsNumeric* function

In many programming situations the user can choose to input data. You have to ensure that the data entered is *valid*. That means that the data must be suitable for the purpose that the task involves. For example we might want the user to input a *number* so that the program can then compare the number input with numbers in a list. Validating input ensures that the program gives correct results and minimises the chances of the program failing.

You can combine another function with **InputBox** to **validate** user input. **IsNumeric** is a function that returns **True** if the input is a number and **False** otherwise.

In this chapter we will build a program that asks the user for a number and tests with the **IsNumeric** function that the input is numeric. If the input is not numeric the program loops until it is by asking the user to input a true number. We will use a **Do … Until** loop to loop and test for a numeric value.

The program will also search for a name once the validated number has been input by the user.

Creating the human–computer interface (HCI)

Open the project **Validate Input** which you will find on your CD-ROM and create the following objects for the HCI of the form:

- two lists, **List1** and **List2** (do not rename these list boxes)
- two labels with captions **Name found** and **Number requested**
- one command button **Get Details and Search**
- another command button **Exit** to quit.

The form should look like Figure 3.27.

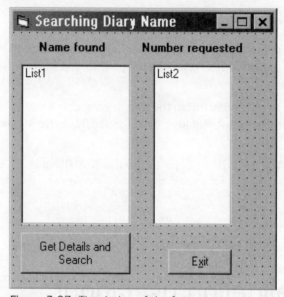

Figure 3.27 The design of the form

Writing the program

You will use the library procedure **TakeInWordsAndNumbers** to ask for pairs of names and numbers. The user will have to input a numeric value before the program will continue. The computer will search the list of numbers to find the number requested using the library procedure **SearchForNumber** and use the position in the list where the number was found to locate the name in the names list. The program will then display them using another procedure, **DisplayNumberSearch**.

Plan for the *ValidateInput* procedure

1 Reserve space for two lists, names and numbers.

2 Get the lists into the computer.

3 Repeat.

4 Ask for a number.

5 Loop until the input is numeric.

6 Search for the number.

7 Display the search result.

Code for the *ValidateInput* procedure

Create a procedure called **ValidateInput** and type this code into it:

```
Dim Names(20), Numbers(20)
TakeInWordsAndNumbers Names(), Numbers(), 5
Do
    SearchNumber = InputBox("Please enter a number to search.")
Loop Until IsNumeric(SearchNumber)
SearchForNumber Numbers(), SearchNumber, 5
DisplayNumberSearch Names(), SearchNumber
```

- The **Dim** statement reserves space for two lists of 20 names and numbers. **Dim Names(20), Numbers(20)** makes the computer reserve space for two lists: a list called **Names** holding up to 20 words and a list called **Numbers** holding up to 20 numbers.
- **TakeInWordsAndNumbers** then fills the lists with the names and telephone numbers you input.
- **SearchNumber = InputBox("Please enter a number to search.")** lets you put a name into the computer. From now on the variable **SearchNumber** in the program will hold whatever you typed in. The **Do … Loop Until** loop ensures only a numeric value is input into the **SearchNumber** variable.

Once space has been reserved in the memory, the procedures listed below can be used:

- **TakeInWordsAndNumbers Names(), Numbers(), 5** was discussed before. It requires three parameters.
- **SearchForNumber Names(), SearchNumber, 5** passes the list of names, the number to be searched for and the length of the list to the procedure. The procedure will look down the list of five numbers until it comes to a number that matches the number you typed in for **SearchNumber** at the **InputBox** above. This will identify the position of the number and will be paired with the name at the same position in the list of names.
- **DisplayWordSearch Numbers(), SearchNumber** will display the number searched for and also the name that is paired with it.

Plan and code for the *Get Details and Search* button

The plan is to call the procedure **ValidateInput**. The code is simply

```
ValidateInput
```

Code for the *Exit* button

As before, the code for the **Exit** button is simply

```
End
```

Running and testing the program

When you run the program it will take in pairs of names and numbers up to the number you specified in the parameter. The program then asks for a number to search the numbers list. The name that corresponds with the number and the number itself are displayed.

Save the project as **Validate Input**.

Now you try

Create a project using the library procedures that you have used in this chapter to write a program to store snooker breaks for a group of players at a tournament. Arrange it so that the program will sort the breaks into descending order and display them along with the players' names on the form. Open the project **Big Break** on your CD-ROM to get you started.

3.8 Select Case ... Case ... End Select

Grades

In this chapter we will again use the computer to make decisions. This time we will use the **Select Case ... Case ... End Select** construction.

Earlier you learned how to use the **If ... Then** and **If ... Then ... Else ... End If** constructions. Why do we need another decision-making construction? Let's examine a situation where we want the computer to calculate grades for a set of marks out of 100 in an exam. We want the program to allocate grades A, B, C, D and E like this:

Marks	Grades
0 to 39	E
40 to 49	D
50 to 59	C
60 to 69	B
70 to 100	A

Learning to use Visual Basic

If we were to use the **If ... Then ... Else ... End If** construction the code would look like this:

```
If mark < 40 Then
    Grade = "E"
Else
    If mark >39 and <50 Then
        Grade = "D"
    Else
        If mark >49 and <60 Then
            Grade = "C"
        Else
            If mark >59 and <70 Then
                Grade = "B"
            Else
                If mark >69 Then
                    Grade = "A"
                End If
            End If
        End If
    End If
End If
```

This construction, even when there are few alternatives for the computer to deal with, is overly complex and it is difficult to follow the logic.

Using the **Select Case ... Case ... End Select** construction, the same logic as above would look like this:

```
Select Case mark
    Case < 40
        Grade = "E"
    Case 40 to 49
        Grade = "D"
    Case 50 to 59
        Grade = "C"
    Case 60 to 69
        Grade = "B"
    Case 70 to 100
        Grade = "A"
End Select
```

This, you will agree, has indeed simplified the logic and length of the code.

We will now try to implement this example to see how the construction works in reality.

Creating the human–computer interface (HCI)

The form will have three list boxes for names, marks and grades, three labels and two buttons. One button will fill the first list with the students' names and the second list with their marks. The second button will calculate the grades using the **Select Case ... Case ... End Select** construction and fill the third list with the grades.

Plan for the form's HCI

1 Create three list boxes for names, marks and grades.
2 Create three labels to document the form.
3 Create two buttons: one to fill the names and marks (caption **Marks**, name **cmdMarks**), and one to calculate the grades (caption **Grades**, name **cmdGrades**).

The form should look like Figure 3.28.

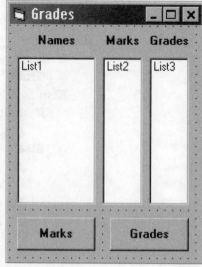

Figure 3.28 The design of the form

Writing the program

The program will calculate the grades from a set of exam marks, allocating grades A to E on the basis of the chart at the beginning of this chapter. All the data will be displayed in the three list boxes which was discussed in the creation of the HCI.

Plan for the *cmdMarks* button

1 Clear **List1**.
2 Fill **List1** with the names of the students.
3 Clear **List2**.
4 Fill **List2** with their marks.

Code for the *cmdMarks* button

Type this code directly into the button's click event procedure:

```
List1.Clear
List1.AddItem "David Mitchell"
List1.AddItem "Craig Donald"
List1.AddItem "Susan Johnstone"
List1.AddItem "Paul Dunlop"
List1.AddItem "Hazel Wilson"
List1.AddItem "Barry Lawson"
List1.AddItem "Allison Haig"
List1.AddItem "June Murray"
List1.AddItem "Pablo Neruda"
List1.AddItem "Peter Stewart"

List2.Clear
List2.AddItem 45
List2.AddItem 56
```

```
List2.AddItem 58
List2.AddItem 84
List2.AddItem 33
List2.AddItem 72
List2.AddItem 91
List2.AddItem 64
List2.AddItem 66
List2.AddItem 75
```

Plan for the *cmdGrades* button

1 Loop for 10 grades
2 Select case of mark in List2
3 If 0 to 39 …
4 … grade it as E and display in List3.
5 If 40 to 49 …
6 … grade it as D and display in List3.
7 If 50 to 59 …
8 … grade it as C and display in List3.
9 If 60 to 69 …
10 … grade it as B and display in List3.
11 If 70 to 100 …
12 … grade it as A and display in List3.
13 End select
14 End the for loop.

Code for the *cmdGrades* button

Type this code directly into the button's click event procedure:

```
For Mark = 0 To 9
Select Case Val(List2.List(mark))
    Case 0 To 39
        List3.AddItem "E"
    Case 40 To 49
        List3.AddItem "D"
    Case 50 To 59
        List3.AddItem "C"
    Case 60 To 69
        List3.AddItem "B"
    Case 70 To 100
        List3.AddItem "A"
End Select
Next Mark
```

We need to use the **For … Next** loop to cycle through the marks in the list box one at a time. As you learned earlier in the course, list boxes are indexed from 0 so the loop starts at 0 and stops at 9. Each value in **List2** is examined in the instruction **Select Case Val(List2.List(mark))**. The **Val** ensures that the data in the list box is treated as a numerical value. Grades are allocated and added to **List3**.

Figure 3.29 shows what the form should look like if your program runs correctly. Click the *Marks* button first, then the *Grades* button. Save the project as **Grades**.

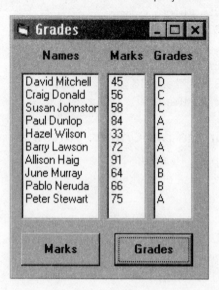

Figure 3.29
The marks grading program running

Grand Prix

Gaining a pole position at a Grand Prix in Formula One is a great achievement. The difference in times between position 1 (pole position) and position 4, say, can be a few hundredths of a second. Computers with very precise telemetric sensors on the cars and around the circuit are used to keep track of the lap times set by the drivers. The timer judge uses computer programs to keep track of the times set by the various drivers trying to set up qualifying times.

We will try to design a project to simulate the timekeeping at a Grand Prix. Again a **combo box** which can be used to display and select information from the screen will prove useful. We will use the **Select Case ... End Select** construction to choose between options in the program.

Creating the human-computer interface (HCI)

Plan for the form *Grand Prix*

1 Open a new form and name it **Grand Prix**.

2 Create a combo box. Visual Basic will give it the name **Combo1**.

3 Create a command button with caption **List Drivers** and name **cmdListDrivers**.

4 Create a command button to prime the start sensor, with caption **Start Run** and name **cmdStartRun**.

5 Create a command button with caption **Show Driver's Time** and name **cmdShowDriversTime**.

6 Create a label to display the time set by the driver. Delete its caption and set its **BorderStyle** to 1 – Fixed Single for that sunken look.

7 Create a command button with caption **Instructions** and name cmdInstructions.

8 Create a command button with caption **Exit** and name cmdExit.

9 Create suitable user-friendly labels to tell the user what's going on.

The form you design should look like Figure 3.30.

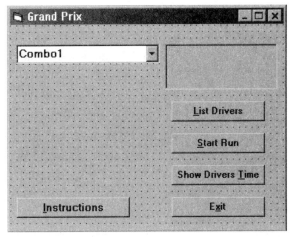

Figure 3.30 The design of the Grand Prix project form

Writing the program

Plan for the *ListDrivers* procedure

The ListDrivers procedure will be called from the **List Drivers** button.

1 Clear the **Combo1** list box.

2 Add six Grand Prix drivers to the **Combo1** list box.

Code for the *ListDrivers* procedure

Double-click the form and create the **ListDrivers** procedure from the **Tools** menu:

```
Combo1.Clear
Combo1.AddItem "Michael Schumacher"
Combo1.AddItem "Rubens Barrichello"
Combo1.AddItem "Ralph Schumacher"
Combo1.AddItem "Juan Pablo Montoya"
Combo1.AddItem "David Coulthard"
Combo1.AddItem "Mikka Hakkinen"
```

Plan for the *StartRun* procedure

1 Select the case of **Combo1**'s text, being:

2 Case Michael Schumacher …

3 … set **Label1**'s caption to "Michael Schumacher has started his lap".

4 Case Rubens Barrichello …

5 … set **Label1**'s caption to "Rubens Barrichello has started his lap".

6 Case Ralph Schumacher …

7 … set **Label1**'s caption to "Ralph Schumacher has started his lap".

8 Case Juan Pablo Montoya …

9 … set **Label1**'s caption to "Juan Pablo Montoya has started his lap".

10 Case David Coulthard …

11 … set **Label1**'s caption to "David Coulthard has started his lap".

12 Case Mikka Hakinnen …

13 … set **Label1**'s caption to Mikka Hakinnen has started his lap".

14 End select

Code for the *StartRun* procedure

Double-click the form and create the **StartRun** procedure from the **Tools** menu:

```
Select Case GrandPrix.Combo1.Text
    Case "Michael Schumacher"
        Label1.Caption = "Michael Schumacher has started his lap."
    Case "Rubens Barrichello"
        Label1.Caption = "Rubens Barrichello has started his lap."
    Case "Ralph Schumacher"
        Label1.Caption = "Ralph Schumacher has started his lap."
    Case "Juan Pablo Montoya"
        Label1.Caption = "Juan Pablo Montoya has started his lap."
    Case "David Coulthard"
        Label1.Caption = "David Coulthard has started his lap."
    Case "Mikka Hakinnen"
        Label1.Caption = "Mikka Hakinnen has started his lap."
End Select
```

Plan for the *ShowDriversTime* procedure

1 Select the case of Combo1's text, being:

2 Case Michael Schumacher …

3 … set Label1's caption to "1:23.028".

4 Case Rubens Barrichello …

5 … set Label1's caption to "1:23.507".

6 Case Ralph Schumacher …

7 … set Label1's caption to "1:23.655".

8 Case Juan Pablo Montoya …

9 … set Label1's caption to "1:23.751".

10 Case David Coulthard …

11 … set Label1's caption to "1:24.802".

12 Case Mikka Hakinnen …

13 … set Label1's caption to "1:24.973".

14 End select.

Code for the *ShowDriversTime* procedure

Double-click the form and create the **ShowDriversTime** procedure from the **Tools** menu:

```
Select Case GrandPrix.Combo1.Text
    Case "Michael Schumacher"
        Label1 = "1:23.028"
    Case "Rubens Barrichello"
        Label1 = "1:23.507"
    Case "Ralph Schumacher"
        Label1 = "1:23.655"
    Case "Juan Pablo Montoya"
        Label1 = "1:23.751"
    Case "David Coulthard"
        Label1 = "1:24.802"
    Case "Mikka Hakinnen"
        Label1 = "1:24.973"
End Select
```

Plan and code for the *Instructions* button

The plan is to set a message box with instructions. The code is:

```
MsgBox "Click the List Drivers button first to fill the Combo box. Select
a driver from the Combo box. Click the Start Run button. The Show
Drivers Time button displays the driver's time."
```

Remember that this must be typed without pressing Enter on your keyboard until the end.

Plan and code for the *List Drivers* button

The plan is to call the procedure **ListDrivers**. The code is:

```
ListDrivers
```

Plan and code for the *Start Run* button

The plan is to call the procedure **StartRun**. The code is:

```
StartRun
```

Plan and code for the *Show Drivers Time* button

The plan is to call the procedure **ShowDriversTime**. The code is:

```
ShowDriversTime
```

Code for the *Exit* button

As before, the code for the **Exit** button is simply

```
End
```

Running and testing the program

Run the program and click the **Instructions** button to see whether the instructions are displayed. Select a driver from the combo box. Click the **Start Run** button and the label should say that the driver selected has started his run. The **Show Drivers Time** button displays the driver's time.

The sequence of screens at runtime should appear as follows. In Figure 3.31 the **Instructions** button has been clicked.

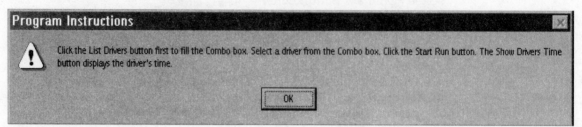

Figure 3.31 The instructions for the user appear when the **Instructions** button is first clicked

In the first part of Figure 3.32 the **List Drivers** button has been clicked and a driver has been selected from the combo box. In the second screenshot the **Start Run** button has been clicked, and in the third screenshot the **Show Drivers Time** button has been clicked.

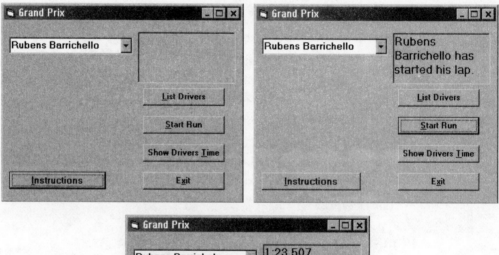

Figure 3.32 Using the Grand Prix program

Save the project as **Grand Prix**.

Your task is to design a project that allows the user to select a recipe by choosing from a combo list box. The ingredients and amounts are displayed in the text box. You can make the textbox as large as you like to accommodate the recipe. Make use of **Select Case ... Case ... End Select** to pick out the correct recipe.

When you create the text box, set its **Multiline** property to **True**. Otherwise the text entered will not wrap around to the next line.

Study the two screen shots of the program running in Figure 3.33 and try to program the command buttons you see.

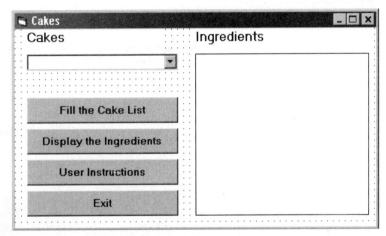

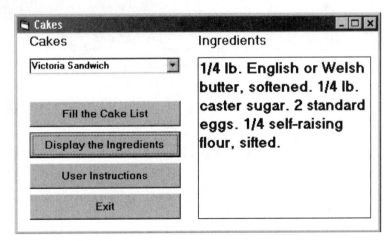

Figure 3.33 The cakes running program should look like this

Adapt the project to display information about five films or five sports teams – or any topic that appeals to you.

Now you try

As you will have noticed, the HCIs we create with the forms are a very important part of projects. The user takes control of the direction the program will take. However sometimes it is not clear with a number of command buttons on the form which button should be clicked first and which buttons will have no effect until the user has performed a prior action.

Take for example the project **Grand Prix**. When the program is first run the two buttons **Start Run** and **Show Drivers Time** have no effect until the **List Drivers** button has been clicked. That would be very frustrating for the user.

Visual Basic allows us to make the user options clearer by using the **Enabled** property available for buttons and other controls. By default the **Enabled** property is set to **True**. When a button's **Enabled** property is set to **False** its text becomes *greyed out*, as in Figure 3.34.

To set the **Enabled** property of the two buttons back to **True**, you will have to provide the enabling code at runtime. Here is how:

```
cmdStartRun.Enabled=True
cmdShowDriversTime.Enabled=True
```

Decide where this code should be placed in your program so that the buttons **Start Run** and **Show Drivers Time** are re-enabled to allow the user access to them after the **List Drivers** button has been clicked.

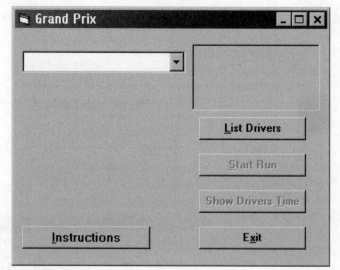

Figure 3.34 The effect of greying out buttons that cannot be used at a certain time in the program's run

3.9 Using Menu Editor

What's on the menu?

Previous chapters have covered programs that involve gathering information from the user. In this chapter you will learn how to present choices to the user just as the professionals do in all the Windows programs that you use. In Windows programs you will find **menus** on the menu bar where related choices are gathered in different menus. Figure 3.35 shows the menu bar from Microsoft Word word-processor.

Learning to use Visual Basic

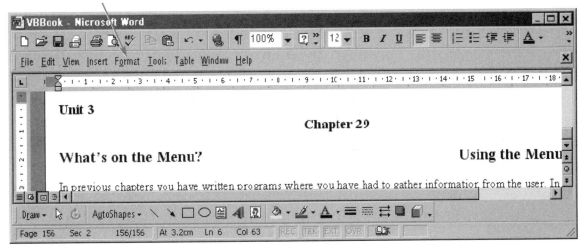

Figure 3.35 The menu bar in MS Word

If you want to add drop-down menus to your forms, use the **Menu Editor**. Let us stay with the menu theme and create a menu bar on a form which will display restaurant dishes along with their culinary descriptions.

Creating the human-computer interface (HCI)

Open a project called **Menus** on your CD-ROM. The form in the project is named **Menus**. The module **Menus.bas** has been added to your project. It contains the descriptions of the dishes you will use in your program.

Once the project is open, click on the form and from the Visual Basic **Tools** menu select **Menu Editor** (or press **Ctrl+E**). When you first open the **Menu Editor** you should see a window as in Figure 3.36.

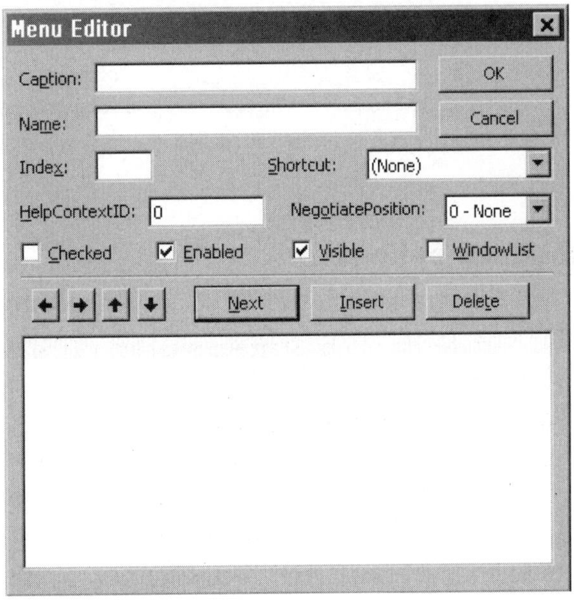

Figure 3.36 The **Menu Editor** window

First item

1 Type **Dishes** into the caption box and **mnuDishes** into the name box, as in Figure 3.37. This name will allow you to use it in Visual Basic code. Leave the other boxes and options as they are.

2 Click the **Next** button. The menu title appears in the menu list box at the bottom of the menu editor and the upper area clears ready for the next menu title. **Dishes** will be the menu title at the top of the form on the menu bar when you run the program.

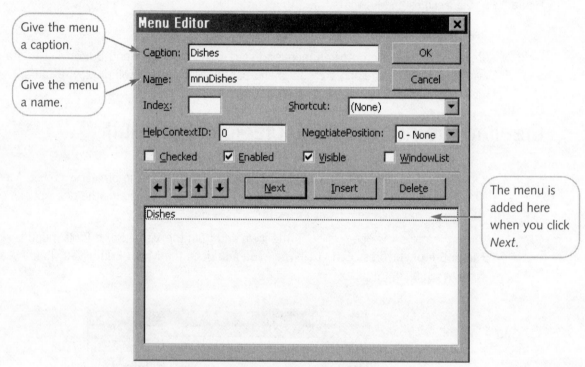

Give the menu a caption.

Give the menu a name.

The menu is added here when you click *Next*.

Figure 3.37 Creating the first menu item, **Dishes**

Sub-menu options

1 Type **Starters** into the caption box and **mnuStarters** into the name box.

2 Click the **Next** button. **Starters** is added to the menu list box underneath **Dishes**. Again the menu editor input area clears ready for the next menu option.

3 We don't want **Starters** to be another menu title along the menu bar at the top of the form. Instead we want it to be a sub-menu option (one that appears when the user clicks on **Dishes**). We need to let Visual Basic know this by *indenting* this option in the menu list. To do this use the arrow button. First click on **Starters** in the menu list to select it, and then click the **right** arrow to indent the option. Figure 3.38 shows the menu editor after you have indented the **Starters** option.

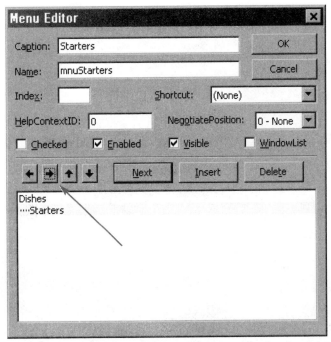

Figure 3.38 The **Starters** option has been indented using the right arrow

You have now managed to create a menu title **Dishes** along the top of the form on the menu bar and by indenting the **Starters** option you have also created a sub-menu option under the **Dishes** title. If you want to see what effect this has in reality, close **Menu Editor** by clicking **OK** and run your program. You should see the **Dishes** menu and be able to pull down the sub-menu to reveal the **Starters** option, as in Figure 3.39.

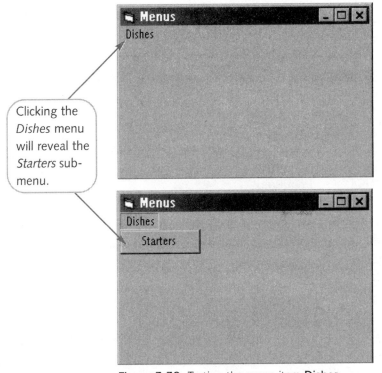

Clicking the *Dishes* menu will reveal the *Starters* sub-menu.

Figure 3.39 Testing the menu item **Dishes**

More sub-menu and sub-sub-menu options

Stop the program running and display **Menu Editor** again from the Visual Basic **Tools** menu. You can continue creating sub-menu options for the **Dishes** menu by repeating the steps above. The other options we want to include under the **Dishes** title are as follows (their captions and their names):

- Accompaniments (**mnuAccompaniments**)
- Indian Breads (**mnuIndianBreads**)
- Tandoori Sizzlers (**mnuTandooriSizzlers**)
- Karahi Dishes (**mnuKarahi**)
- Birryani Dishes (**mnuBirryani**)
- Tandoori Speciality (**mnuTandoori**)
  …Chicken or Lamb Tikka Bhoona (**mnuBhoona**)
  …Chicken or Lamb Tikka Garam Masala (**mnuMasala**)
- Kormas (**mnuKormas**)
- Balti Dishes (**mnuBalti**).

Add all the above options under the **Dishes** menu. *Remember to indent all the options.* When you come to the two options Chicken or Lamb Tikka Bhoona and Chicken or Lamb Tikka Garam Masala you must give them a **double indent**, as they will be sub-menus for the **Tandoori Speciality** sub-menu option.

Any time that you want to see how your menu creation is coming along, click **OK** on the menu editor to put it away and run the program and pull down the **Dishes** menu. If you notice any menu options that are along the menu bar rather than under the **Dishes** menu, it means that you have forgotten to indent them in **Menu Editor**. In that case stop the program running and display **Menu Editor** again. Then select the option(s) and indent using the right arrow button.

Second main menu item

We want to have another menu title along the menu bar at the top of the form to end the program. To do this, open **Menu Editor** (or if you have it already displayed, click **Next** to clear the boxes).

Type **Exit** into the caption box and **mnuExit** into the name box. Do not indent this option as you want it to appear at the top of the form along the menu bar to the right of **Dishes**.

Creating the form

1 Create a list box and size it as you see in Figure 3.40. Set its font style to bold 14pt.

2 Create three labels and place them exactly as you see in Figure 3.40. **Label1** should have its **BorderStyle** set to 1 – Fixed Single for that sunken look. Set the fonts for all labels to bold 14pt.

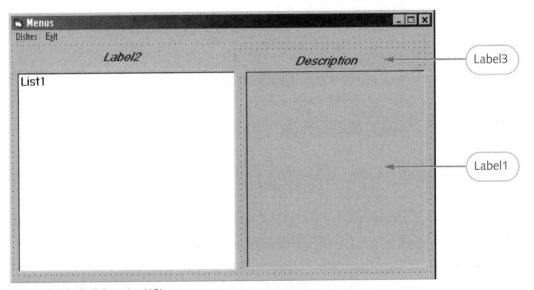

Figure 3.40 Building the HCI

Writing the program

The program will allow the user to select Indian dishes from a pull-down menu. A list box will display the dishes and a label will give a description of the category of dish selected. All you have to do in the way of programming is to ensure that each menu option calls a library procedure that was loaded when you opened the project **Menus**. The program also has a menu option to end the program.

Plan for the *Dishes* menu

1 mnuStarters calls the **Starters** procedure.
2 mnuAccompaniments calls the **Accompaniments** procedure.
3 mnuIndianBreads calls the **IndianBreads** procedure.
4 mnuTandooriSizzlers calls the **Sizzlers** procedure.

5 mnuKarahi calls the **Karahi** procedure.

6 mnuBirryani calls the **Birryani** procedure.

7 mnuTandoori

   ... mnuBhoona calls the **Bhoona** procedure.

   ... mnuMasala calls the **GaramMasala** procedure.

8 mnuKormas calls the **Korma** procedure.

9 mnuBalti calls the **Balti** procedure.

Code for the *Dishes* menu

Each menu option calls a corresponding procedure via its click event procedure. In design mode, click each menu option and its click event will be displayed. Type the call to the procedures as you see below:

```
Private Sub mnuStarters_Click()
    Starters
End Sub
Private Sub mnuAccompaniments_Click()
    Accompaniments
End Sub
Private Sub mnuIndianBreads_Click()
    IndianBreads
End Sub
Private Sub mnuTandooriSizzlers_Click()
    Sizzlers
End Sub
Private Sub mnuKarahi_Click()
    Karahi
End Sub
Private Sub mnuBirryani_Click()
    Birryani
End Sub
Private Sub mnuBhoona_Click()
    Bhoona
End Sub
Private Sub mnuMasala_Click()
    GaramMasala
End Sub
Private Sub mnuKormas_Click()
    Korma
End Sub
Private Sub mnuBalti_Click()
    Balti
End Sub
```

Plan and code for the *Exit* menu

mnuExit will end the program. The code for the **Exit** menu is simply

```
End
```

Type that command in the menu's click event window.

Running and testing the program

The program typically displays the dishes which comprise a category when an option is selected. Figure 3.41 shows the form when the **Karachi** menu option is selected.

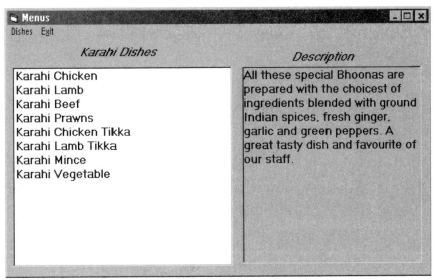

Figure 3.41 The contents of the Karahi option with the program running

Note that the library procedures deal with what happens in the list box and labels on the form. Test all the menu options to make sure that the calls to procedures are working correctly.

Make sure that the sub-menu options for the **Tandoori Speciality** menu are also working properly when you select them, as in Figure 3.42.

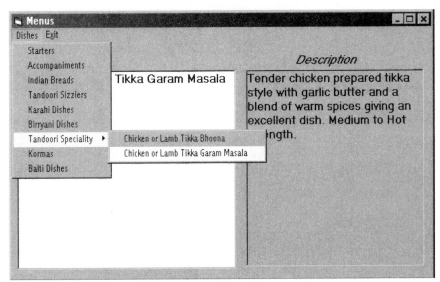

Figure 3.42 Using the sub-menus

Save the project when it is working correctly.

Now you try

Add another menu **Price** to the menu bar. The user should be able to choose a dish from the menu and its price appears in a label on the form. Adjust the form's HCI with the extra controls required. You will need two more labels, one for the caption **Price** and one to hold the price of the dish. There is an example in Figure 3.43.

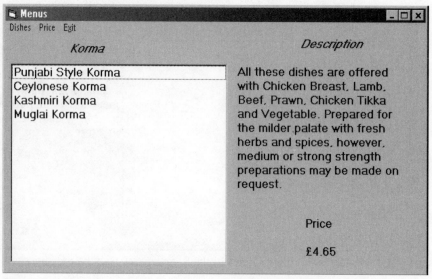

Figure 3.43 How you can display the price for individual dishes

In *each* of the click events for the options you will need to insert extra code. An example is:

```
Sub mnuTandooriDishes_Click()
    Sizzlers
    Label4.Caption="£5.50"
End Sub
```

Since you saved the last project **Menus** you will have the module **Menus** added already. Have a look at the various procedures within the module **Menus**. This will allow you to see which procedures you need to call when the user clicks options in the **Price** menu.

Now you try

1 Create a project using menus to display in list boxes the names of music groups and their songs.

2 Use menus to display in list boxes the names of sport teams and their players. Also add a label to this project so that you can display information about the teams and players.

3 Choose a topic that interests you and give it the 'menu' treatment!

3.10 Using Do While ... Loop

Testing conditions

You have learned to use the **Do ... Loop Until** loop to test the condition of a password being correct. The condition in a **Do ... Loop Until** loop is tested at the end of the loop. Let us remind ourselves of how it works:

```
Do
    ID = InputBox("Please enter your password.")
Loop Until ID = "Let me in"
MsgBox "You have been given access."
```

Note that the condition is tested in the line **Loop Until ID = "Let me in"** so that the instruction in the loop **ID = InputBox("Please enter your password.")** will be carried out at least once and the loop can only be exited and access granted if the condition is met.

In this chapter you will learn how to use a **Do While ... Loop** which provides a different way to process a condition. Let's examine the same password test using the **Do While ... Loop**:

```
ID = InputBox("Please enter your password.")
Do While ID <> "Let me in"
    ID = InputBox("Please re-enter your password.")
Loop
MsgBox "You have been given access."
```

The test is made at the start of the loop which means that the instruction in the loop **ID = InputBox("Please re-enter your password.")** may never be carried out if the condition is not met.

Think of a real-life situation where a driver of an electric train has to push on a handle to keep the train in motion. The train will keep moving as long as the handle is pushed forward. The handle is spring loaded to return to the stop position if the driver releases pressure. This 'dead man's handle' could be implemented using a **Do While ... Loop** like this:

1 Pressure on handle is greater than 0 (start the train).

2 **Do while** pressure on handle is greater than 0.

3 Keep train moving.

4 **Loop**.

5 Stop train (pressure on handle is 0 so cut power and apply brakes).

As soon as the driver applies pressure to the handle the train moves forward and while pressure continues to be applied the train continues to move. The loop executes continuously to test the condition *pressure must be greater than 0*. The loop is exited if the pressure ever falls to 0, in which case the train is automatically brought to a halt by the brakes.

You have already used **Do ... Loop Until** to test for a valid (numerical) input from the user. You can also use the **Do While ... Loop** in your programs to test for valid input.

First project: Days in the month

We will create a project to ask the user for a month of the year and test for a valid numerical input that is in the range of 1 to 12. The program will then tell the user how many days there are in the month entered. We will use the **Do While ... Loop** to validate the input.

Creating the human–computer interface (HCI)

1 Create three labels on the form. Give Label1 the caption '**Your month has**'. Label2 should be blank, so delete its caption and give it that sunken look, as before. Label3's caption should be '**days.**'.

2 Create a button to hold the code in its click event procedure. Make its caption '**Enter Month**' and name it **cmdEnterMonth**.

The form should look like Figure 3.44.

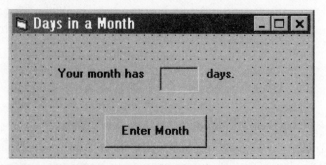

Figure 3.44 The design for the form

Writing the program

The program will use an **array** to hold the number of days in the months. When the button is clicked the user is asked to enter a month number from 1 to 12. A **Do While ... Loop** will test for a valid input in the range of 1 to 12. The number of days in the month will be displayed in a label on the form.

Plan for the *cmdEnterMonth* button

1 Declare an array to hold the numbers of days in the months.

2 Set 12 array elements to days in the month corresponding to an index number.

3 Get a month number from the user.

4 Loop while the number is not in the 1 to 12 range, and ...

5 ... display an error message.

6 Get a valid month number from the user.

7 End the loop.

8 Set the label to the number of days in the chosen month.

Code for the *cmdEnterMonth* button

The required code is:

```
Dim MonthDays(12) As Integer
MonthDays(1) = 31
MonthDays(2) = 28
MonthDays(3) = 31
MonthDays(4) = 30
MonthDays(5) = 31
MonthDays(6) = 30
MonthDays(7) = 31
MonthDays(8) = 31
MonthDays(9) = 30
MonthDays(10) = 31
MonthDays(11) = 30
MonthDays(12) = 31
MonthNumber = InputBox("Please enter a month (1 to 12)")
Do While MonthNumber < 0 Or MonthNumber > 12
MsgBox "The number must be in the range of 1 to 12."
MonthNumber = InputBox("Please re-enter a month (1 to 12).")
Loop
Label2 = MonthDays(MonthNumber)
```

Running and testing the program

Run the program and click the **Enter Month** button. The program should accept a number between 1 and 12 only. If a valid number is entered the program should display the number of days in the month in the label on the form, as in Figure 3.45.

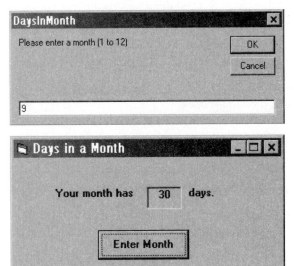

Figure 3.45 What should happen when you run the program

Save the program as **Days in Month**.

Second project: Lift control

You are now going to create a program to control a lift using a **Do While ... Loop**. A lift in a building has a safety maximum weight of 850kg that it can hold, and will not operate with a weight above the safety maximum. The program to control the operation of the lift will allow more people to enter the lift and the door to close while the weight is less than or equal to 850kg. Every time another person enters the lift the extra weight will be added to the total weight so far. However, if the limit of 850kg is exceeded the program will speak a synthesized warning and display a message that the last person to enter should get out.

The lift control program can use a **Do While ... Loop**. The logic of the program will look like this:

1 **Do while** the total weight is less than or equal to 850kg ...

2 ... allow more weight into lift.

3 **Loop**.

4 Give a warning and display a message.

So the **Do While ... Loop** statement tests a condition – that the total weight is less than or equal to 850kg. While this condition is **True** the loop repeats, and the processing continues within the loop – totalling the weight and allowing more people to enter. If at any time the weight exceeds 850kg the condition becomes **False**. The processing moves outside the loop and continues with the next instruction after the loop.

The synthesized warning will be implemented using the Visual Basic **Beep** keyword that is onomatopoeic in function and uses the computer's speaker.

Creating the human–computer interface (HCI)

This is the plan for the **Lift** program which makes sure that the lift doors will close only while the weight does not exceed 850kg. Pay close attention to the naming of objects as their names are crucial to the operation of the program.

1 Set the form's name property to **frmLift** and its caption to **Lift Control**.

2 Create a button to open the lift door, with caption **Open Lift Door** and name **cmdOpenLiftDoor**.

3 Create a button to close the lift door, with caption **Close Lift Door** and name **cmdCloseLiftDoor**.

4 Create a button to add a person to the lift, with caption **Next Person** and name **cmdNextPerson**.

5 Create a button to remove a person, with caption **Remove Person** and name **cmdRemovePerson**.

6 Create a button to exit the program, with caption **Exit** and name **cmdExit**.

7 Create two image objects.

8 Create a label, with caption blank and name **LiftWeight**.

9 Create a label, with caption **Weight in lift 850kg max**, to document the interface.

This form has quite a few objects, so look at the chart to help you set the properties.

Object	Property	Setting
Form1	Name: Caption:	FrmLift Lift Control
Command1	Name: Caption:	cmdOpenLiftDoor Open Lift door
Command2	Name: Caption:	cmdCloseLiftDoor Close Lift Door
Command3	Name: Caption:	cmdNextPerson Next Person
Command4	Name: Caption:	cmdRemovePerson Remove Person
Command5	Name: Caption:	cmdExit Exit
Label1	Name: Caption:	LiftWeight Blank
Label2	Name: Caption:	Label2 Weight in lift 850kg max

Have a look at the finished form in Figure 3.46 and adjust the properties to match as closely as possible what you see.

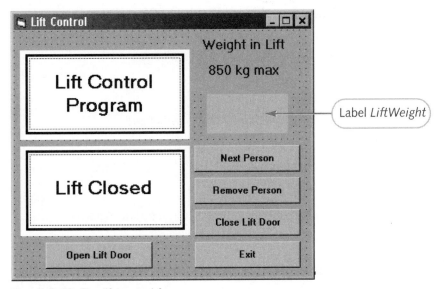

Figure 3.46 The lift control form

The two image objects hold **bitmap** images which can be created using the Windows program called **Paint**. If you do not want to create your own bitmaps you will find some on your CD-ROM in a folder called **Lift**. Follow these steps to place a bitmap into an image object:

1 Once you have created the image object, select it and press **F4** to bring up its property window.

2 Set the **Picture** property to the bitmap by browsing for it after you click the ellipsis button, as in Figure 3.47. The image object should now have the bitmap loaded into it.

3 Carry out the same steps to create the second image on the form. The second image will toggle between being visible and invisible within the program code.

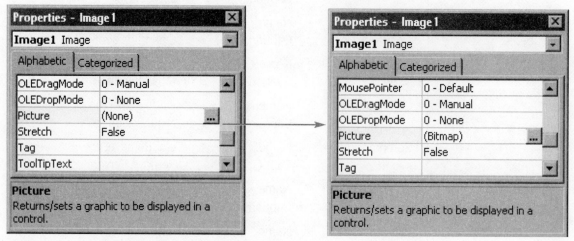

Figure 3.47 Setting the properties of an image object

Writing the program

Each button, except for the **Exit** button, will call a procedure that you will create.

Plan for the procedure *CloseDoor*

The procedure called by the **Close Lift Door** button will require most attention as it uses the **Do While ... Loop**. The plan is:

1 **Do while** weight in lift is less than or equal to 850kg ...

2 ... allow **image2** to be visible and ...

3 ... leave the procedure.

4 End **loop**

5 Beep.

6 Set a message with a warning that there is too much weight in the lift.

> You can view the structure diagram version of this plan on your CD-ROM.

Code for the procedure *CloseDoor*

Create a procedure **CloseDoor** and type this code into it:

```
Do While Val(LiftWeight) <= 850
    Image2.Visible = True
    Exit Sub
Loop
Beep
MsgBox "There is too much weight in the lift! Please remove a person."
```

The two lines of code, **Image2.Visible = True** and **Exit Sub**, will be executed only if the weight in the lift is less than or equal to 850kg. **Image2.Visible = True** reveals the **Lift Closed** sign. **Exit Sub** means that processing can leave the loop as the condition has been met. If the condition is not met then the warning message "There is too much weight in the lift! Please remove a person." will come up.

Plan for the procedure *AddPerson*

1 Make **image2** invisible.

2 Add 85kg to the weight in the lift (for the sake of the simulation we will allow 85kg as the weight of one person).

Code for the procedure *AddPerson*

Create a procedure **AddPerson** and type this code into it:

```
Static Sub AddPerson()
    Image2.Visible = False
    LiftWeight = Val(LiftWeight) + 85
End Sub
```

It is important that you add the keyword **Static** to the procedure declaration. This will ensure that the variable values will be preserved on subsequent calls to the procedure. Here we are interested in the **LiftWeight** variable.

The line **LiftWeight = Val(LiftWeight) + 85** adds 85kg to the weight already in the label variable **LiftWeight**. The **Val** function makes sure that, whatever the label caption happens to be, it is the numeric value we are given. With **Image2.Visible = False** we make invisible the sign 'Lift Closed'.

Plan for the procedure *RemovePerson*

1 Make **image2** invisible.

2 Subtract 85 from the weight in the lift.

Code for the procedure *RemovePerson*

Create a procedure **RemovePerson** and type this code into it:

```
Static Sub RemovePerson()
    Image2.Visible = False
    LiftWeight = Val(LiftWeight) - 85
End Sub
```

Again it is important that you add the keyword **Static** to the procedure declaration. This will ensure that the variable values will be preserved on subsequent calls to the procedure. Here once more we are interested in the **LiftWeight** variable.

The line **LiftWeight = Val(LiftWeight) - 85** subtracts 85kg from the weight already in the label variable **LiftWeight**. The **Val** function makes sure that, whatever the label caption happens to be, it is the numeric value we are given. With **Image2.Visible = False** we make invisible the sign 'Lift Closed'.

Plan and code for the procedure *OpenDoor*

We want to make **image** 2 (the sign 'Lift Closed') invisible. Create a procedure **OpenDoor** and type this line of code into it:

```
Image2.Visible = False
```

Code for the *Exit* button

You do not need to create a procedure for this button. Just type **End** into its click event. It will quit the program for the user.

Plan and code for the buttons

Each button should call the appropriate procedure from its click event. Double-click each button to get its click event code window. Type each procedure name into the buttons' click events like this:

- in the **Next Person** button type **AddPerson**
- in the **Remove Person** button type **RemovePerson**
- in the **Close Lift Door** button type **CloseDoor**
- in the **Open Lift Door** button type **OpenDoor**.

Running and testing the program

You need to run the program to test that each button calls its procedure. Test the program as follows:

1 Run the program. The form should appear as in Figure 3.48.

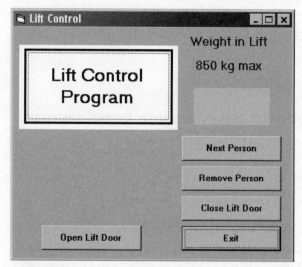

Figure 3.48 How the program should open

2 Click the **Next Person** button seven times and then click the **Close Lift Door** button. Is the computer adding up the weights properly? (7 × 85 = 595!) Does the 'Lift Closed' image appear?

3 Click the **Next Person** button another four times and then click the **Close Lift Door** button. A warning message should come up, as in Figure 3.49.

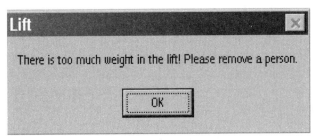

Figure 3.49 Lift control warning message

4 Click **OK** to the message. Click the **Remove Person** button once to resolve the problem of too much weight!

5 Now click the **Close Lift Door** button and the 'Lift Closed' image should appear, as in Figure 3.50.

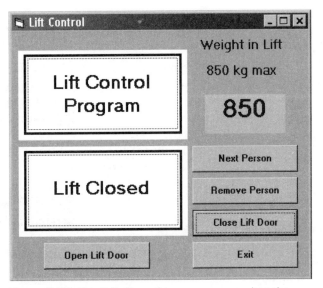

Figure 3.50 The 'Lift Closed' image appears when the problem of overweight has been resolved

Save the project as **Lift**.

Now you try

1 You are saving up to buy a bicycle which costs £320. Every week you deposit money you have earned into a savings account. Design a dialogue box with a command button which when clicked asks you how much you want to deposit. The program should keep you informed of the amount of money you have managed to save so far. When you have deposited £320 or more the program should tell you that you can now buy your bicycle.

2 Design a dialogue box with four command buttons. Each button when clicked will ask a general knowledge question. If the answer is wrong the question should be repeated. Use **InputBox** to ask the questions.

Help
Hotkeys

Give your mouse a rest and make the keyboard do more work! You can do this by creating **hotkeys** for activating the buttons on your forms.

The hotkey is actually part of the **caption** on the button. The way to achieve this is to place an **ampersand** (&) *in front of the letter you want to act as the hotkey*. Use the caption property to do this.

The letter chosen as the hotkey is *underlined*, as you will have noticed in many of the forms pictured in this book. The hotkey will be activated by **Alt + the letter underlined**. Obviously you must not duplicate any underlined letters on a single form.

Figure 3.51 shows some examples, related to the lift control project in this chapter.

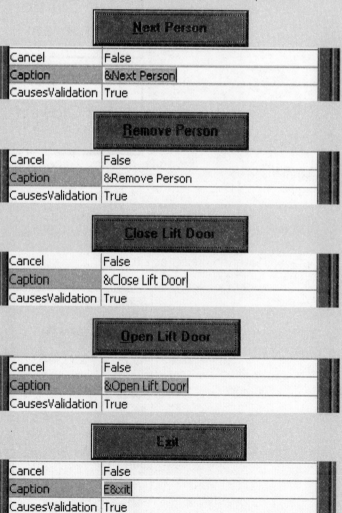

Figure 3.51 Modifying the caption property to create a hotkey.

3.11 Formatting output

Café Bistro pay-roll

The owner of Café Bistro would like a program to work out the pay for his employees and to tell him how much the total wages bill is every week. We will try to create a project to do this.

The form for the project will display the name, job title, pay per hour, normal hours worked, overtime and final pay for each employee, as well as the total wages bill.

It will be necessary to have three command buttons: one button each to fill the names, jobs and pay per hour lists.

Creating the human–computer interface (HCI)

1 Create eight labels to document the form, with captions **Pay-roll**, **Name**, **Job**, **Pay per hour**, **O/T**, **Final Pay**, **Hrs** and **Total Wages Bill**.

2 Create a label and set its name property to **WagesBill**.

3 Create six list boxes and set their name properties to **NamesList**, **JobList**, **PayList**, **HoursList**, **OvertimeList** and **FinalPayList**.

4 Create three command buttons, with captions **Employees**, **Calculate Pay** and **Exit**, and with names **cmdEmployees**, **cmdCalculatePay** and **cmdExit**.

Make sure that for each list box you set its **name** property to the name given above. This is important as those names are used in the program code.

Have a look at Figure 3.52 and design your form similarly. Now that you have learned how to create **hotkeys**, implement them in your design. Also arrange that the **Calculate Pay** button is greyed when your program first runs.

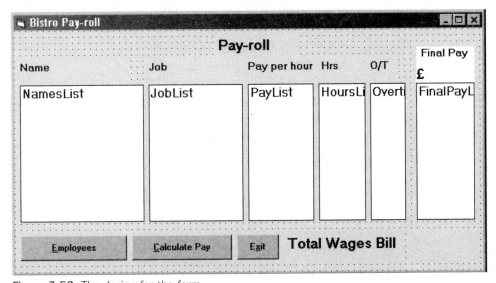

Figure 3.52 The design for the form

Writing the program

Plan for the procedure *EmployeeDetails*

1 Enable the **Calculate Pay** button.

2 Clear the **NamesList** box.

3 Add items (AddItems) to the **NamesList** box: 'Judith Ashford', 'Peter Stewart', 'Joseph Knwokedi', ' Margaret Rose', 'Alex Babalola', 'Mary Alencar', 'Olegario Lucas', and 'Joshua Heinz'.

4 Clear the **JobList** box.

5 Add items to the **JobList** box: 'Manager', 'Head Chef', 'Sous Chef', 'Commis Chef', 'Head Waiter', 'Head Waitress', 'Sommelier', 'Dish-washer'.

6 Clear the **PayList** box.

7 Add items to the **PayList** box using the **Format** function:
Format(12.5, "£#,00.00")
Format(10.6, "£#,00.00")
Format(8.5, "£#,00.00")
Format(7, "£#,00.00")
Format(8, "£#,00.00")
Format(8, "£#,00.00")
Format(8.9, "£#,00.00")
Format(4.6, "£#,00.00")

Code for the procedure *EmployeeDetails*

Create a procedure called **EmployeeDetails** and type the following code into it:

```
Sub EmployeeDetails()

'Name of workers
cmdCalculatePay.Enabled = True
NamesList.Clear
NamesList.AddItem "Judith Ashford"
NamesList.AddItem "Peter Stewart"
NamesList.AddItem "Joseph Knwokedi"
NamesList.AddItem "Margaret Rose"
NamesList.AddItem "Alex Babalola"
NamesList.AddItem "Mary Alencar"
NamesList.AddItem "Olegario Lucas"
NamesList.AddItem "Joshua Heinz"

'Job description
JobList.Clear
JobList.AddItem "Manager"
JobList.AddItem "Head Chef"
JobList.AddItem "Sous Chef"
JobList.AddItem "Commis Chef"
JobList.AddItem "Head Waiter"
JobList.AddItem "Head Waitress"
```

```
JobList.AddItem "Sommelier"
JobList.AddItem "Dish-washer"

'Rate per hour
PayList.Clear
PayList.AddItem Format(12.5, "£#,00.00")
PayList.AddItem Format(10.6, "£#,00.00")
PayList.AddItem Format(8.5, "£#,00.00")
PayList.AddItem Format(7, "£#,00.00")
PayList.AddItem Format(8, "£#,00.00")
PayList.AddItem Format(8, "£#,00.00")
PayList.AddItem Format(8.9, "£#,00.00")
PayList.AddItem Format(4.6, "£#,00.00")
End Sub
```

List boxes can look untidy when intended currency values are added to the list but do not line up within the list box. The **Format** function with the symbols described here can help. Study the coding for this project and learn to make use of **Format** in your future projects.

Help

Here is information about the **Format** function used in the program:

Symbol	Description
0	Digit placeholder – prints a trailing or a leading zero in this position, if appropriate
#	Digit placeholder – never prints trailing or leading zeros
.	Decimal placeholder
,	Thousands separator
– + $ ( ) space	Literal character – characters are displayed exactly as typed into the format string

Although here we have created our own **Format** string following the rules above, Visual Basic supplies the system formats that come with Windows. So here for example you could use the *Currency* format like this:

```
Format(12.5, "Currency")
```

Notice that the word *Currency* must be within quotes or an error will occur. Other formats you can use are "General Number", "Fixed", "Standard", "Percent", and "Scientific".

If we were to implement the code for the PayList list box with this easy format it would look like this:

```
PayList.Clear
PayList.AddItem Format(12.5, "Currency")
PayList.AddItem Format(10.6, "Currency")
PayList.AddItem Format(8.5, "Currency")
PayList.AddItem Format(7, "Currency")
PayList.AddItem Format(8, "Currency")
PayList.AddItem Format(8, "Currency")
PayList.AddItem Format(8.9, "Currency")
PayList.AddItem Format(4.6, "Currency")
```

Plan for the procedure *CalculatePay*

1 Clear the **HoursList** box.

2 Clear the **OvertimeList** box.

3 Clear the **FinalPayList** box.

4 Set the **WagesBill** label to 0.

5 Loop for eight workers.

6 Get **NormalHours** with **InputBox** and prompt.

7 Add **NormalHours** to **HoursList**.

8 Get **OverTime** with **InputBox** and prompt.

9 Add **OverTime** to **OvertimeList**.

10 Set **FinalPay** to (**NormalHours** * **PayList** row) + (**OverTime** * **PayList** row / 2).

11 Add **FinalPay** with **Format** to **FinalPayList**.

12 Set **WagesBill** with **Format** to **WagesBill** + **FinalPay**.

13 End the for loop.

Code for the procedure *CalculatePay*

Create a procedure called **CalculatePay** and type this code into it:

```
Sub CalculatePay()
'Type CalculatePay into this button

'Calculate pay and wages bill
HoursList.Clear
OvertimeList.Clear
FinalPayList.Clear
WagesBill = 0
For worker = 0 To 8 - 1
    NormalHours = InputBox("Please enter number of normal hours
                    worked for " & Chr$(13) & NamesList.List(worker))
    HoursList.AddItem NormalHours
    OverTime = InputBox("Please enter number of hours overtime
                    worked for " & Chr$(13) & NamesList.List(worker))
    OvertimeList.AddItem OverTime
    FinalPay = Val((NormalHours * PayList.List(worker)) + (OverTime *
                                        PayList.List(worker) / 2))
    FinalPayList.AddItem Format$(FinalPay, "£#,000.00")
    WagesBill = Format$((WagesBill + FinalPay), "£#,000.00")
Next worker

End Sub
```

Note that the first item in a list has an index of 0 so we have to take one away from the loop to be able to make use of the control variable *worker*.

Running and testing the program

Run the program and the form is displayed as in the top part of Figure 3.53. Note that the **Calculate Pay** button is greyed so that the user is invited to use the **Employees** button.

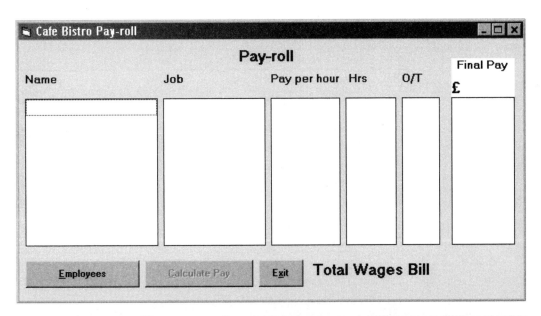

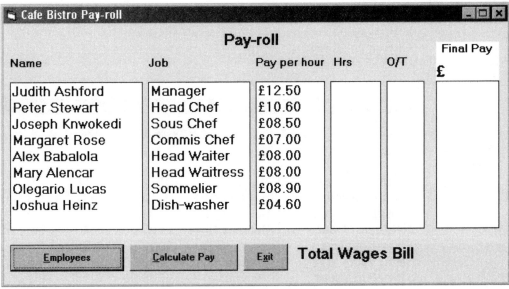

Figure 3.53 The wages program in use

When the **Employees** button is clicked, the name, job and pay per hour lists are filled and the **Calculate Pay** button is enabled, as in Figure 3.53.

Click the **Calculate Pay** button and the program prompts for the number of normal hours and overtime hours worked for the first employee, as in Figure 3.54.

Payroll
Please enter number of normal hours worked for Judith Ashford
OK
Cancel
36
Payroll
Please enter number of hours overtime worked for Judith Ashford
OK
Cancel
5

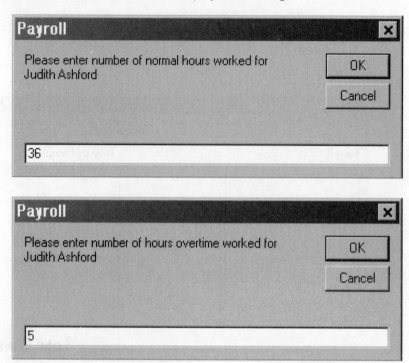

Figure 3.54 The **Calculate Pay** prompt

When all employees have been processed the program displays the normal and overtime hours worked and the total pay for each employee and the total wages bill, as in Figure 3.55.

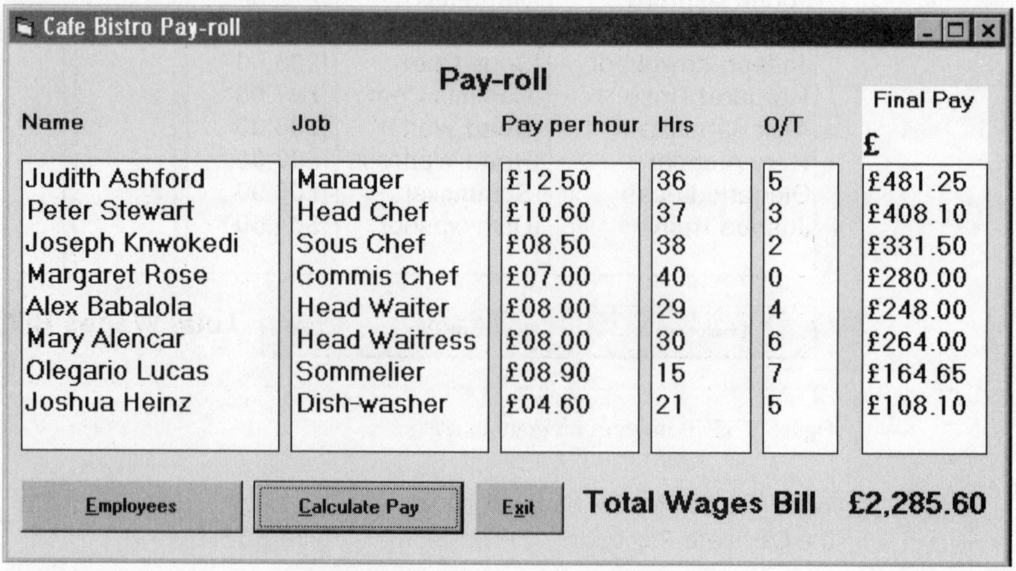

Cafe Bistro Pay-roll
Pay-roll
Name
Job
Pay per hour
Hrs
O/T
Final Pay £
Judith Ashford | Manager | £12.50 | 36 | 5 | £481.25
Peter Stewart | Head Chef | £10.60 | 37 | 3 | £408.10
Joseph Knwokedi | Sous Chef | £08.50 | 38 | 2 | £331.50
Margaret Rose | Commis Chef | £07.00 | 40 | 0 | £280.00
Alex Babalola | Head Waiter | £08.00 | 29 | 4 | £248.00
Mary Alencar | Head Waitress | £08.00 | 30 | 6 | £264.00
Olegario Lucas | Sommelier | £08.90 | 15 | 7 | £164.65
Joshua Heinz | Dish-washer | £04.60 | 21 | 5 | £108.10
Employees
Calculate Pay
Exit
Total Wages Bill £2,285.60

Figure 3.55 The total wages bill has been calculated and displayed

Save your project as **Payroll**.

Create a food and drinks dispenser project where the user clicks an **Image** control and its click event procedure displays a picture appropriate to the choice. You will find the images you require in a folder called **Snacks** on the CD-ROM. Make sure you use the **Format** function so that the prices in the list box line up properly.

Figures 3.56 and 3.57 will give you some ideas.

You can decide to have these controls either as *images* or *command buttons*. In either case it is the *click event* procedure that you want to use.

This is an *Image* control that displays different pictures depending on selection.

Hint: To get an image onto a button its *Style* property must be set to *1-Graphical* and then you can set its *Picture* property as required.

Figure 3.56 Design for the form

Three items were clicked. The last image clicked was 'Pizza' and the OK button was clicked for the total.

Figure 3.57 The program running

Dice game

It is useful when programming to be able to generate **random numbers**. We may just want to create a dice game, and what's more random than throwing dice! Visual Basic supplies the function **Rnd** that generates random numbers to our specification. For example, **6 * Rnd** will return a number between **0** and **5**, so if we want random numbers between **1** and **6** inclusive we can give the computer the command:

> (6 * Rnd) + 1

We add 1 to whatever number the computer comes up with, which in this case will be between 0 and 5. We don't want a zero, so adding 1 will avoid this! If **Rnd** returns a 5 we will add 1 to it so we will also get sixes.

Rnd does not always return a whole number, so we could get numbers like 2.1885632. That is no use for our purpose, so we need to force Visual Basic to give us whole numbers. Our command will need to be:

> Int(6 * Rnd) + 1

The **Int** function makes sure that we get only integers (whole numbers) generated.

Using Randomize

Randomize uses the computer's system clock to create a truly random starting point, or 'seed' for the **Rnd** statement used in the **Dice** procedure. Without **Randomize** the program is likely to produce the same pattern of numbers every time the program is run. The **Form_Load ()** procedure is a good place to put the command **Randomize**, as it will run automatically every time the program executes.

Jargon buster

Seed – The principle behind using a seed is to supply the **Rnd** function with a new starting point each time it is called. Using the number of seconds since midnight supplied by the computer's system clock guarantees that the seed will be different each time. **Randomize** is the Visual Basic keyword that uses the system clock for this purpose.

Creating the human–computer interface (HCI)

Now that we have a method to get random numbers we can turn our attention to creating the dice game. Our game will be quite simple. The user will throw two dice for a maximum of three throws. The two numbers thrown will be displayed in two labels on the form. The user at the start of the program will be asked to stake a sum of money. If a throw generates a double then the stake is doubled. If no doubles are thrown within the three throws the user loses his or her stake. The program should also show the amount won by the player, or a 'sorry' message if the stake is lost.

Plan for the form

Create the following objects on the form:

- eight labels to document the form
- one text box (name it **Stake**)
- two labels to show the throws made (name them **Die1** and **Die2**)
- one label to show how much has been won (name it **Winnings**)
- one button to call the **Dice** procedure (set its **Style** property to 1 – Graphical so that you can change its colour, and set its **BackColor** property to red).

Pay close attention to setting the **Name** property for the text box and label objects exactly as specified above, otherwise your program will not run correctly.

Try to design your form to look similar to what you see in Figure 3.58.

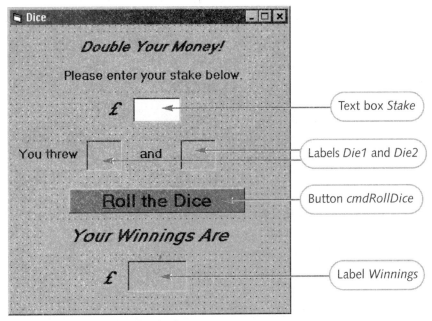

Figure 3.58 The design for the form

Writing the program

Plan for the procedure *Dice*

1 Set number of throws to number of throws + 1.
2 If(1) the number of throws is greater than two:
3 ... If(2) the number of **Doubles** equals 0 then ...

4	... give the player a sorry message and ...
5	... set **Winnings** to 0 and ...
6	... set **Throws** to 0 and ...
7	... exit the procedure and ...
8	... end if(2).
9	... Give the player a game-over message.
10	... Set **Stake** to 0 and ...
11	... set **Throws** to 0 and ...
12	... set **Winnings** to 0 and ...
13	... exit the procedure.
14	End if(1).
15	Set a value for **Die1** with **Rnd**.
16	Set a value for **Die2** with **Rnd**.
17	If(3) **Die1** equals **Die2** then ...
18	... set **Winnings** to **Winnings** so far plus the **Stake** times 2 and ...
19	... increment the **Doubles** variable by 1.
20	End if(3).

Code for the procedure *Dice*

Create a procedure **Dice** and type this code into it:

```
Static Sub Dice()

Throws = Throws + 1

If Throws > 2 Then
    If Doubles = 0 Then
        MsgBox "Oh well, you lose this game. Have another go!"
        Winnings = 0
        Throws = 0
        Exit Sub
    End If
    MsgBox "Game over!"
    Stake = 0
    Throws = 0
    Winnings = 0
    Stake.SetFocus
    Exit Sub
End If

Die1 = Int(6 * Rnd) + 1 'Generate a random value between 1 and 6
Die2 = Int(6 * Rnd) + 1 'Generate a random value between 1 and 6
If Die1 = Die2 Then
    Winnings = Val(Winnings) + Val(Stake) * 2
    Doubles = Doubles + 1
End If

End Sub
```

Plan and code for the procedure *Form_Load*

The plan is to set the seed with **Randomize**. The code for the procedure is:

```
Randomize
```

Plan and code for the *cmdRollDice* button

The button will call the **Dice** procedure. Its code is:

```
Dice
```

Running and testing the program

Run the program and enter a stake into the text box and then click the **Roll the Dice** button. Figures 3.59 and 3.60 show the results for an unsuccessful throw and a successful one.

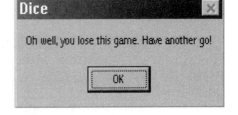

Figure 3.59 An unsuccessful result for a throw

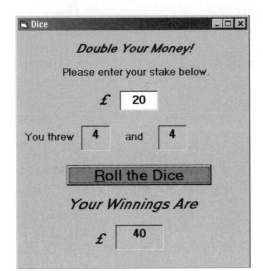

Figure 3.60 A successful result for a throw

Now you try

Create a project to allow a player to guess a number that the computer generates with the **Rnd** function.

- The player should be told that the number is within a certain range.
- As guesses are made the program should report either 'too low' or 'too high'.
- Decide how many chances the player will have to guess the number (the greater the range the more chances should be given).
- The program should also give the number of guesses taken if the player guesses the number.

Now you try

Supertask

Improve the dice game project designed in this chapter by adding graphic feedback to the player. The project should display image frames **bitmaps** for the six different faces of the dice. You will need to create bitmaps using the MS Paint application, or use the designs provided in **Dice Faces** on your CD-ROM.

Disable the two label controls **Die1** and **Die2** so they are invisible on the form, and draw images on the form on top of the dice labels. Figure 3.61 shows an example of what you might aim for.

Figure 3.61 Two bitmap images have been added to make the form more attractive

Hints

- Create six bitmap images using MS Paint. Save them as DieFace1, DieFace2 etc.
- Use **Select Case** to test **Die1** and **Die2** for the value that **Rnd** has given them and set the images to **LoadPicture** as appropriate.
- The syntax for **LoadPicture** is:

    ```
    Image1 = LoadPicture("Path to the bitmap file on your disk")
    ```

Using strings

We humans are very different from computers, you may be glad to hear! We live and communicate with each other in a world of language, where we use words and phrases to pass messages to each other. Computers are not language machines at all. They are designed as number processing machines. Any task that a computer carries out is done by manipulating binary patterns of zeros and ones (0s and 1s). If this is the case, how then do we manage to get the computer to understand words?

A solution to this is to give each character in a word a **code**. Because computers use binary we give the characters a binary code. The computer can then use binary codes to try to understand what we are communicating with words.

In programming, when characters are combined together to form words and phrases we call them **strings**. So a string is a collection of characters. Here are some examples of strings:

- "Bananas"
- "Shut that door!"
- "c"
- "Where's my hat?"
- "30 September 2003"
- "22".

String values must have quote marks (" ") around them. This is essential as it tells Visual Basic that the characters in the quotation are of **type** *string*. Characters without quotation marks are considered either as variables or as part of the programming language. Even though "22" looks like a numerical value you cannot perform arithmetical calculations such as multiplication or addition with it. You can even have an empty string – that is, a string with no characters at all!

You can have fun with strings. You can compare them, reverse them, chop them up and put them together again. Visual Basic supplies many functions to do these things for you.

Any character or symbol that you can display on your computer has a different code. The name of the code is **ASCII**, which stands for 'American Standard Code (for) Information Interchange'. So for example, the lower-case letter 'a' has an ASCII code of 97 and uppercase 'A' has ASCII code 65. Even the **Enter** key has a code: it is 13. We are lucky because we don't need to memorise the codes. The computer always remembers them.

Jargon buster

Computers are not intelligent! – Always bear in mind that humans communicate with language. When, for example, we ask a question the inflexion in our voice will tell someone that we are asking a question. That level of natural and intelligent communication is not possible yet between computers and humans. When dealing with computers we have to go down to the level of the ASCII character and see what the codes are. Does the **string** that the user just typed in have a question mark at the end? Or does the phrase contain an interrogative word – like 'What' or 'Where' – at the start? We then create programs using the functions supplied in Visual Basic to help us manipulate the words and phrases – the strings! Strings and their functions are an interface between us with our language and the computers with their number processing programs and ASCII character sets.

Now you try

In the first project in this chapter you will create a program to code a string. The user will be able to type in a word or phrase and the program will turn it into a coded message.

Before you start the project, have some fun by using a couple of programs to display ASCII codes and to decode ASCII codes and display characters.

1 Run the program called **KeyPressedDemo** supplied on your CD-ROM. It will tell you the code for any character you care to type in (Figure 3.62).

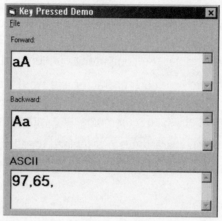

Figure 3.62 Running KeyPressedDemo

2 The **ASCIIDecoder** program also supplied on the disc will decode any ASCII code you care to type in (Figure 3.63). Use this decoder program to decode the message 65, 83, 67, 73, 73, 32, 105, 115, 32, 97, 32, 99, 111, 100, 101, 46.

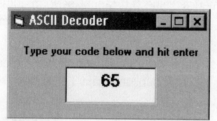
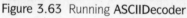
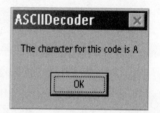

Figure 3.63 Running ASCIIDecoder

First project: How long is a string?

To see how a program uses strings we will create a simple project that uses a very useful function that Visual Basic supplies called **Len** (short for length). What **Len** does is return the number of characters in a string. For example, a command like Len("Where is my hat?") will give you the answer 16 – don't forget to count the spaces and the question mark!

Creating the human–computer interface (HCI)

1 Set the form's caption to **How long is a string?**
2 Create a text box to allow the user to type in a string.

3 Create a button with caption **How Long?** and name **cmdHowLong**.

4 Create a label to tell the user where to type the string.

The form should look like Figure 3.64.

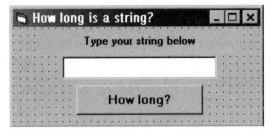

Figure 3.64 The design for the form

Writing the program

Plan for the *cmdHowLong* button

1 Set the variable **LengthOfString** to the number of characters in **Text1** using the **Len** function.

2 Set a message that displays the length of the string.

Code for the *cmdHowLong* button

The required code is:

```
LengthOfString = Len(Text1)
MsgBox "You typed in a string that is " & LengthOfString & " characters
                                                                  long"
```

Whatever the user types into the text box makes up the string. When the button is clicked the function **Len** will return the number of characters in the string and its length will be displayed.

Running and testing the program

Run the program, type something into the text box and then click the button. The number of characters in the text box should be displayed in a message box, as in Figure 3.65.

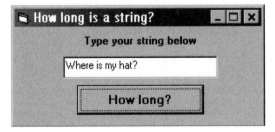 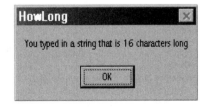

Figure 3.65 Type various things into the text box to test your program

Save your program as **Len**.

Second project: Code it

We will create a project to code words. When a word or phrase is coded it means that the characters in the message have been changed using a certain rule. For example, a simple rule could be that we shift forward three places in the alphabet and allocate that character to the letter in question. If we were to apply that rule, a 'd' would become a 'g' and an 'l' would become an 'o', and so on. Here is a list of coded words:

- edqdqdv
- rudqjhv
- ohprqv
- dssohv

This list was created using the **CodeIt** program you will now create. If you have sensitive information, then coding can protect it against hackers and other breaches of security.

Creating the human–computer interface (HCI)

Before you start to design the project, from the CD-ROM open the **Code It** project that contains some library functions you will need for this program.

Plan for the *Code It* form

1 Create a text box to accept a word.

2 Create a first label to display the coded word. Set its **BackColor** to black and **ForeColor** to white.

3 Create a command button whose click event calls the procedure **CodeIt**. Name it **cmdCodeIt**.

4 Create labels to document the form for the user.

Your form should look like Figure 3.66.

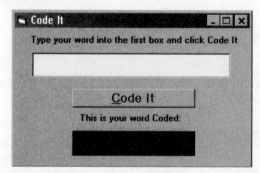

Figure 3.66 The design for the form

Writing the program

As you saw from the HCI design, we plan to allow the user to type in the word to be coded into the text box at the top of the form. When the **Code It** button is clicked then the procedure **CodeIt** will be run.

Once we get the word from the user we will take each letter in turn, use **Asc** to find its ASCII code value, add a number like 3 to the ASCII value and then turn this new number back into a letter using **Chr**.

How do we get the length of the word to start with? Visual Basic's very useful function called **Len** can do that for us. You have seen, for example, that a command like **Len**("Where is my hat?") will give you the answer 16.

The characters on your keyboard are given ASCII codes inside the computer. You will see in our program **CodeIt** that the function **Asc** returns the code for a character. For example **Asc**("A") will return the ASCII code 65 (the code for A is 65).

You will also see that the function **Chr** returns the character for a given ASCII code. For example, the command **Chr(65)** will return the character A because 65 is the ASCII code for A.

Plan for the *CodeIt* procedure

1 Get the number of letters in the word in **Text1** box.

2 Loop for the number of letters in the word.

3   Find the first letter.

4   Work out the code for the letter.

5   Build coded word.

6   Strip first letter from word.

7 End the for loop.

Code for the procedure *CodeIt*

Create a procedure **CodeIt** for your project and then type this code into it (the functions OnlyFirstLetter and AllButFirstLetter will already be in this project for you to call):

```
Sub CodeIt()
Length = Len(Text1)
UnCoded = Text1
For Letter = 1 To Length
    FirstLetter = OnlyFirstLetter(UnCoded)
    'The OnlyFirstLetter function finds the first letter in your word
    Number = Asc(FirstLetter)
    'Asc finds the ASCII code
    NewNumber = Number + 3
    NewLetter = Chr(NewNumber)
    'Chr turns the code back into a letter
    Coded = Coded + NewLetter
    UnCoded = AllButFirstLetter(UnCoded)
    'The AllButFirstLetter function strips the first letter from the word
    'before the next repetition of the loop, so that the next letter can be
    'coded; this is repeated until the whole word is done
Next Letter
Label1.Caption = Coded
End Sub
```

Obviously it is not essential for you to type in the comment lines.

Understanding the *CodeIt* procedure

Read again through the Visual Basic code we have used for the **CodeIt** procedure. Make sure you understand each line of code. The explanations are given below in square brackets.

```
Sub CodeIt()
```

[The procedure codes a word or phrase by taking each letter and giving it another ASCII code and displaying the word or phrase again in its coded form.]

```
Length = Len(Text1)
```

[The variable **Length** is set to the number of characters entered into the text box using **Len**.]

```
UnCoded = Text1
```

[We set the **UnCoded** variable to the contents of the text box.]

```
For Letter = 1 To length
```

[The **For ... Next** loop loops for the number of characters in the text box **Length**.]

```
FirstLetter = OnlyFirstLetter(UnCoded)
```

[The variable **FirstLetter** is set to the first letter of the variable **UnCoded** using the function **OnlyFirstLetter**.]

```
Number = Asc(FirstLetter)
```

[The variable **Number** is set to the ASCII code of the **FirstLetter** variable using the **Asc** function.]

```
NewNumber = Number + 3
```

[We want to give the letter a new code so we add 3 to the existing code and set NewNumber to this.]

```
NewLetter = Chr(NewNumber)
```

[It is now possible to create a new character using the **Chr** function with the parameter NewNumber.]

```
Coded = Coded + NewLetter
```

[The variable **Coded** each time round the loop is built up letter at a time into the new coded string.]

```
UnCoded = AllButFirstLetter(UnCoded)
```

[Next time round the loop we want to deal with the next character in the word, so we use the function **AllButFirstLetter** to strip the first character from the string **UnCoded**. This means that the function **OnlyFirstLetter** earlier in the loop is dealing with the next character in the string.]

```
Next Letter
```

[Let's do all that again if required!]

```
Label1.Caption = Coded
```

[Display the new coded string on the form in a label.]

```
End Sub
```

Understanding the *CodeIt* procedure: a dry run

Let us do a dry run of this procedure using a three-letter string. We'll use the word *fun* and follow its progress through the procedure to see how it is re-coded and the values of the variables as we step through the loop. We will use three columns when in the For … Next loop as we can anticipate that the loop will be done three times.

Length = Len(Text1)	Length = 3		
UnCoded = Text1	Uncoded = 'fun'		
For Letter = 1 To Length			
	Times round the loop		
	First	*Second*	*Third*
First Letter = OnlyFirstLetter(UnCoded)	FirstLetter = 'f' UnCoded = 'fun'	FirstLetter = 'u' UnCoded = 'un'	FirstLetter = 'n' UnCoded = 'n'
Number = Asc(FirstLetter)	Number = 102	Number = 117	Number = 110
NewNumber = Number + 3	NewNumber = 105	NewNumber = 120	NewNumber = 113
NewLetter = Chr(NewNumber)	NewLetter = 'i'	NewLetter = 'x'	NewLetter = 'q'
Coded = Coded + NewLetter	Coded = 'i'	Coded = 'ix'	Coded = 'ixq'
UnCoded = AllButFirstLetter(UnCoded)	UnCoded = 'un'	UnCoded = 'n'	UnCoded = '' (empty)
Next Letter Label1.Caption = Coded	After the loop is exited the new coded word "ixq" is displayed in the label.		

Running and testing the program

Run the project and test it with the word 'fun'. When you click the **Code It** button the label should display the new coded word 'ixq', as in Figure 3.67.

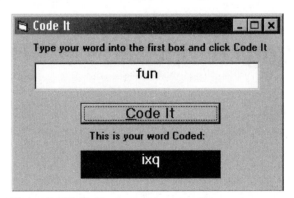

Figure 3.67 The code program running

Save the project as **CodeIt**.

Now you try

1 It is easy to change your program so that it can decode the coded messages. Think how you could do this. You will need to change your HCI to make the decoding program user-friendly.

2 Decode this message: Surjudpplqj#lv#ixq$. Use the program you created in task 1 above. Figure 3.68 shows you how.

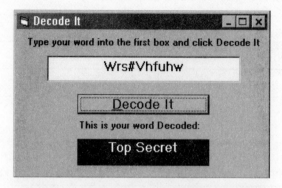

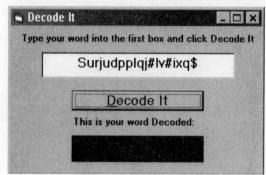

Figure 3.68 Using your decoding program

3 Decode the words listed near the top of page 166.

4 If you add 32 to the ASCII code of an upper-case letter you get its lower-case equivalent. Write a program to change a word from upper-case to lower-case.

5 What is your name in ASCII code?

3.14 Logical operators (NOT)

Palindrome

'A man, a plan, a canal – Panama!' If you read that backwards you get the same phrase. Easier ones are 'madam' and 'evil rats on no star live'. These are called *palindromes*. If you care to browse the Internet for palindromes you will find many more. Simple examples are: bob, dad, wow, deed, radar, civic. You can write a program to tell you whether a word is a palindrome or not.

In this chapter you are going to study the use of an **operator**. The operator **NOT** is often used to test a comparison in a conditional statement. It will serve our purpose as we test to see whether a word is a palindrome. To test for a palindrome in a computer program you need to carry out three programming tasks:

1 *Get a word from the user.* Use **InputBox** to do this.

2 *Reverse the word input by the user.* Use the function **StrReverse** to turn the word backwards.

3 *Test the word input with itself, reversed.* Use the **NOT** operator to return **True** or **False**. The **NOT** operator turns what is true into false and what is false into true. So if the word is a palindrome and reversed it is **Pal** then the statement **Pal = Word** will be true. If the word is not a palindrome then the statement **Pal = Word** will be false. We can then use an **If … Then … End If** construction to test for the truthfulness or otherwise of the statement **NOT(Pal = Word)**.

Creating the human–computer interface (HCI)

1 Create a text box and name it **MyWord**.

2 Create a command button to call the procedure **Palindrome**. Make its initial 'T' a *hotkey*.

3 Create a label to display the result of the test with a suitable message (palindrome or not). Set its **BorderStyle** to 1 – Fixed Single for that sunken look.

The finished form is shown in Figure 3.69.

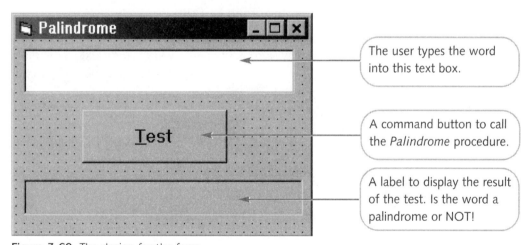

Figure 3.69 The design for the form

Writing the program

The plan for the program is to use the **NOT** operator in a conditional statement which will mean that the instructions in the conditional statement will be done only if the operation that **NOT** performs on the condition actually turns it **True** – which means that in reality the condition **(Pal = Word)** must be **False**. Yes, **NOT** does seem to turn logic on its head!

Plan for the procedure *Palindrome*

1 Set the variable **Pal** to the reverse of the **Word**.
2 If the result of the comparison of **Pal** and **Word** is not true, then ...
3 ... display in the label the message 'Not a palindrome'.
4 Exit the **Palindrome** procedure.
5 End If.
6 Display in label 'Yes that's a palindrome. Well done!'

Code for the procedure *Palindrome*

Create a procedure **Palindrome** at the form level. Arrange that **MyWord** is passed as a parameter to the procedure. **MyWord** is the actual parameter and **Word** is the formal parameter:

```
Sub Palindrome(Word)
    Pal = StrReverse(Word)
        'The StrReverse function reverses the letters of Word and places
                                        the result in the variable Pal

        If Not (Pal = Word) Then
            Label1.Caption = "Not a palindrome"
            Exit Sub
            'If Pal is not the same as Word then display message and
                                                exit procedure

        End If
        Label1.Caption = "Yes that's a palindrome. Well done!"
End Sub
```

Plan and code for the *Test* button

The plan is to call the procedure **Palindrome** and pass the variable **MyWord** to it as a parameter. Remember **MyWord** is the name you gave to **Text1** box when you created your design. Here we use it as the actual parameter. The code is simply

```
Palindrome MyWord
```

Running and testing the program

Run the program and type a word into the **MyWord** text box, as in Figure 3.70. Click the **Test** button and see whether it is a palindrome.

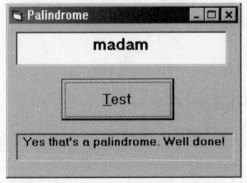

Figure 3.70 Testing the **Palindrome** program

Save your program as **Palindrome**.

Jargon buster

True or false: Boolean type (see *Boolean* on your CD-ROM)

In Visual Basic we can set a variable to hold one of two values, **True** or **False**. We are telling Visual Basic that sometimes the variable might be true and at other times it might be false. The variable in fact takes on a **Boolean** type.* It has a binary existence, sometimes worth a **1** (True) and at other times worth a **0** (False) just like in binary arithmetic. True and False are Visual Basic keywords.

All you have to do to make a variable Boolean is to set it either to True or to False. We need True and False in programming so that we can test conditions in coding. Here is an example of True and False being used to set a variable, **OlderThanSixteen**:

```
OlderThanSixteen = False
UserAge = InputBox("Please enter your age.")
If UserAge > 16 Then
    OlderThanSixteen = True
End If
```

The variable **OlderThanSixteen** starts off being False but if the user enters an age greater than 16 then the variable **OlderThanSixteen** will be set to True in the **If … Then** condition.

Later in the program the user wants to apply for a driving licence:

```
If OlderThanSixteen = True Then
    MsgBox "You may apply for a driving licence."
Else
    MsgBox "Sorry, you must be older than 16 to apply for a driving licence."
End If
```

Visual Basic remembers whether or not **OlderThanSixteen** was set to True earlier in the program. If the variable was set to True then the first message is displayed and if not the second message is displayed.

Because **OlderThanSixteen** is of Boolean type we can also use it without the **'= True'** part of the coding in this example, like this:

```
If OlderThanSixteen Then
    MsgBox "You may apply for a driving licence."
Else
    MsgBox "Sorry, you must be older than 16 to apply for a driving licence."
End If
```

Another way to use the Boolean type is in an expression like this:

```
If UserAge > 16 = True Then
    MsgBox "You may apply for a driving licence."
Else
    MsgBox "Sorry, you must be older than 16 to apply for a driving licence."
End If
```

*George Boole (1810–1864) was a mathematician who developed a method of describing logical problems. His algebra of logic used symbols like **AND**, **OR** and **NOT**. His work became the basis for the design of logic circuits that modern computers use.

3.15 Logical operators (AND)

User name AND password

If you use a computer network at school or college you will be familiar with logging in by typing your *user name* and *password*. If you type in the correct user name but the wrong password then access to the computer system is denied. The same is true if the password is correct but the user name is wrong, or if both are wrong. So the logic of it is like this:

- wrong user name *and* correct password = no access
- correct user name *and* wrong password = no access
- wrong user name *and* wrong password = no access
- correct user name *and* correct password = access!

So the **AND** operator works by taking two inputs. It returns **True** only if both inputs are true. It returns **False** in every other case. Your school or college network operating system runs a program that uses the **AND** operator as described above.

 Now you try

To study how the **AND** operator is used, run and list the program **PasswordOperator** supplied on your CD-ROM. Here is part of the code:

```
If UserName = "Lynda" AND Password = "Secret" Then
    MsgBox ("Welcome, Lynda! Ready to start your PC?")
```

Note that the program on the disc allows only two users on to the network. Add yourself to the users who are allowed to log in! After looking at Figure 3.71 create a different **bitmap** picture to appear for your own login screen. Good luck with getting in!

Figure 3.71 Lynda's and Paul's login screens when they have successfully entered their user names and passwords

3.16 Logical operators (OR)

Input validation: age

It is very important for computers to be reliable by giving correct results. This can be possible only if the input is itself *valid*. A program that asks for your age is expecting you to enter a numerical value, and any characters that do not represent a number should be rejected by the computer.

In an earlier chapter you saw that the computer stores characters as **ASCII codes**. The numerical characters lie in the range from ASCII code 48 to ASCII code 57. If a user when asked for his or her age enters a character with an ASCII code that is outside the range 48 to 57 (>57 *or* <48 – greater than 57 *or* less than 48) then the user will be asked to re-enter. **OR** is a logical operator that will allow us to test the validity of the codes entered.

We will need a method to step through each character of the string that is entered by the user, look at each character in turn, and decide whether its code is valid or not. There is a string function **Mid** that will let us look at characters in a string. It takes three parameters:

- the string in question
- where you want to start looking from
- the number of characters you want to include from that position

like this:

> C = Mid(UserInputString, Character, 1)

Here **C** would receive the result of the **Mid** function being called. **Character** is a variable that would set the position to begin looking from. We use **1** as the third parameter because we want to look at only one character at a time.

We can find out what ASCII code **C** has by using the function **Asc**. **Asc(C)** will return the code for **C**. We could do a test like:

> If Asc(C) > 57 OR Asc(C) < 48 Then

You have already met the string function **Len** that returns the number of characters in a string. So along with a **For … Next** loop we have all we need to check the user's input for validity. We are ready to plan a procedure to ask for an age and check for valid characters.

Creating the human-computer interface (HCI)

1 Create a text box for the user to enter an age. Name it **UserInput**.

2 Create a command button. Set its caption to **Test Age** and its name to **cmdTestAge**.

3 Create a label to document the form.

Figure 3.72 shows the form in design mode.

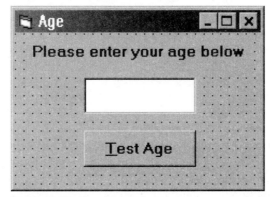

Figure 3.72 The design for the form

Writing the program

Plan for the procedure *Validate*

1 Set a valid variable to True.

2 Loop for the length of the user's input.

3 Set C to a character in the string using **Mid**.

4 If(1) the ASCII code for C is greater than 57 or less than 48, then …

5 … set the valid variable to False.

6 End If(1).

7 End Loop for.

8 If(2) the valid variable is False, then …

9 … inform user of invalidity with MsgBox

10 … else thank the user and reset focus to the text box.

11 End if(2).

Code for the procedure *Validate*

Create a procedure called **Validate** and type this code into it:

```
Sub Validate()
'This procedure tests what the user inputs into the text box UserInput
'and asks the user to re-enter if any non-numeric characters are
'detected

Valid = True
For Character = 1 To Len(UserInput)
    C = Mid(UserInput, Character, 1)
    If Asc(C) > 57 Or Asc(C) < 48 Then
            Valid = False
    End If
Next Character
If Valid = False Then
    MsgBox "Please re-enter. An invalid character was detected."
    UserInput.SetFocus
Else
    MsgBox "Thank you for your valid input."
    UserInput.SetFocus
End If
End Sub
```

Plan and code for the *cmdTestAge* button

The plan is to call the **Validate** procedure. The code for the button is:

```
Validate
```

Plan for the procedure *Form_Load*

1 Show the form.

2 Put the cursor into the text box **UserInput**.

Code for the procedure *Form_Load*

The required code is:

```
Form1.Show
UserInput.SetFocus
```

Understanding the *Validate* procedure

Read again through the Visual Basic code we have used for the **Validate** procedure. Make sure you understand each line of code. The explanations are given below in square brackets.

```
Sub Validate()
```

[The **Validate** procedure tests input into a text box, **UserInput**, to ensure that all the characters that make up the string are numbers. If any other characters are found the user is asked to re-enter the input.]

```
Valid = True
```

[We set the Boolean variable **Valid** to True before we go into the loop.]

```
For Character = 1 To Len(UserInput)
```

[The **For … Next** loop will be done for the number of characters in the user input.]

```
C = Mid(UserInput, Character, 1)
```

[The C variable is set to **Next Character** in the string using the **Mid** function.]

```
If Asc(C) > 57 Or Asc(C) < 48 Then
    Valid = False
End If
```

[If the ASCII code of the C variable has a code that is greater than 57 or less than 48 then **Valid** is set to false. Loop once again if there are still characters to deal with.]

```
Next Character
If Valid = False Then
    MsgBox "Please re-enter. An invalid character was detected."
```

[If the **Valid** variable has been previously set to false, then tell the user that an invalid character was found and get the user to re-enter. Put the cursor back into the text box.]

```
    UserInput.SetFocus
Else
    MsgBox "Thank you for your valid input."
```

[Otherwise thank the user for a valid input.]

```
    UserInput.SetFocus
```

[Put the cursor back into the text box.]

```
End If
End Sub
```

Running and testing the program

Testing with a full set of test data

We will test the program with both numbers and letters to see that only valid input is accepted.

Our **Age** program needs **numeric** data in the ASCII range of codes, 48 to 57 inclusive. Testing needs to be carried out in a logical manner to ensure that the program is robust in coping with any type of data and does not fail and is also reliable by outputting correct results, where an ASCII code greater than 57 or less than 48 should be rejected.

When you compile a set of data to test a program you choose the items for input so that the program can deal with all inputs. With a program that is intended to process numeric input, programmers use three standard tests on the program, using three types of data. The three types of data used for testing are **extreme**, **normal** and **invalid**. How do these different data items test the program? We will use a sample set of data to demonstrate how the program will be tested.

Extreme test

First we choose numbers that will test the program at the extremes of the conditions set. These extreme data will test the conditions:

```
If Asc(C) > 57 OR Asc(C) < 48 Then
    Valid = False
```

Greater than 57 or less than 48 are the conditions, so we would choose **0** (ASCII code 48) and **9** (ASCII code 57). These data items are at the extremes of the conditions. The numbers 0 and 9 should therefore be accepted by the program (Figure 3.73).

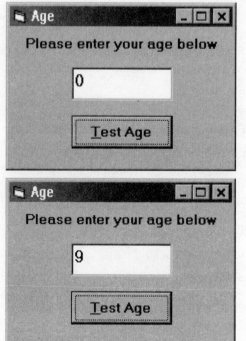

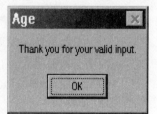

Figure 3.73 Testing the program with extreme values

Normal test

Second we choose numbers that will test the program with normal data. These normal data will test the same conditions:

> If Asc(C) > 57 OR Asc(C) < 48 Then
> > Valid = False

Let's say we choose the two numbers **3** and **7**. They are not greater than ASCII code 57 nor less than ASCII code 48, so we are OK and the program should not fail but should accept the data (Figure 3.74). The ASCII codes for 3 and 7 are 51 and 55 respectively.

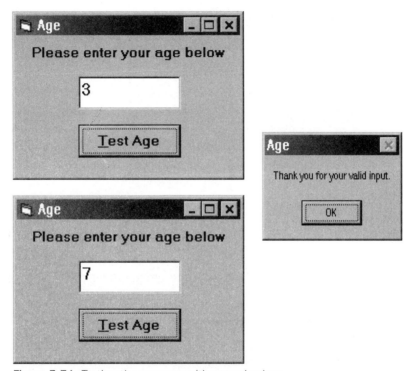

Figure 3.74 Testing the program with normal values

Invalid test

Third we choose data that are invalid according to the conditions. These **invalid** data will again test the same conditions:

> If Asc(C) > 57 OR Asc(C) < 48 Then
> > Valid = False

Invalid data is anything that is not a number because then the data would lie outside the ASCII code range 48 to 57. In the **Age** program we could use **t** and **F** as test data because any text can be used for this invalid (or exceptional) test.

In the invalid test you should also use a string with valid and invalid data to see whether the program can pick out invalid data among valid data. You can test **Age** using the strings **k2** and **C5**, for example (Figure 3.75 on the next page).

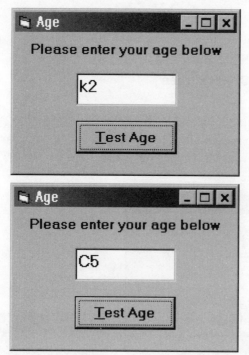

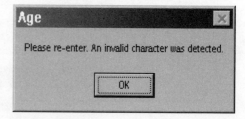

Figure 3.75 Testing the program with invalid values

Checking validity with the *KeyPressedDemo* program

You can use the **KeyPressedDemo** program that you used to find out the ASCII codes in an earlier chapter. You will find the program in a folder of the same name on the CD-ROM.

For example, if you type 0 or 9 into the program the program will display ASCII codes 48 and 57 respectively. So in the above we *are* testing the extremes of the conditions.

Using the **KeyPressedDemo** program, if you type k2 or C5 into the program the program will display ASCII codes 107 for the k and 67 for the C respectively (Figure 3.76). So the

program **Age** correctly rejects the string with data that is outside the ASCII range of codes 48 to 57.

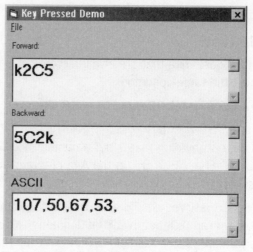

Figure 3.76 Using the **KeyPressedDemo** program to check for valid values

Save the program as **Age** when you have satisfactorily completed all the tests.

Learning to use Visual Basic

Jargon buster

Mid – The **Mid** function can pick out a character or another string in a given string. As explained in the text, it takes three parameters. The first parameter is the string being dealt with. The second parameter is a variable or value that sets the position that will be the starting position to begin picking from. The third parameter is a variable or value that sets the length of the new string. Here is an example.

Let's say the initial string is the title of the book *One Hundred Years of Solitude*. Then the following programming statements would set the **NewString** variable to *Solitude*:

```
BookString = "One Hundred Years of Solitude"
NewString = Mid(BookString, 22, 8)
```

Note that the **Mid** function also has a form where it only takes two parameters. If the third parameter is omitted then the string picked out is formed from the value set by the second parameter to the end of the string. So, Mid(BookString, 13) would return the new string "Years of Solitude".

Now you try

1 Change the **Age** program so that it asks for the months of the year and displays them in a list box. The program should accept only letters and no numerical characters or any other keyboard characters. You will need to find out which are the ASCII codes for the alphabet (upper-case and lower-case).

2 As was stated at the start of this chapter, validation is important. You might want to investigate how you could use Visual Basic's **IsNumeric** function to solve the problem for the **Age** program.

Now you try

In Unit 4, in the sections 'Testing' and 'Runtime evidence', you can study examples of preparing test data for project work and assessment purposes. Use those sections and what you have learned in this chapter to help you create test data, when you are asked to do so in a task.

3.17 Drag and drop

Postie

You will be used to clicking buttons and menus in Windows programs. You can also **drag and drop**. To drag and drop, the user holds down the mouse button, drags an object from one position to another, and then lets go the mouse button to drop the object or issue a command.

This can be a useful facility to give users. They can then do things like dragging text from one place to another in word processing or remove objects from the screen by putting them in a bin. I am sure you can think of many more examples where drag and drop is used in Windows programs.

There are three important tasks that you have to carry out to enable drag and drop:

- *Enable drag and drop for the object.* Visual Basic needs to know which objects are going to be dragged. To add drag and drop capability to an object you must set its **DragMode** property to 1 by using program code or the Properties window.
- *Select a drag icon.* Visual Basic normally uses a rectangle to represent the object as it is being dragged, but you can change this with a different drag icon if you want. Set the **DragIcon** property to an icon or bitmap from program code or the Properties window.
- *Write a **DragDrop** or **DragOver** event procedure for the target object.* Write event code in the **DragDrop** or **DragOver** event procedure for the object that will receive the dragged object, either by being dropped on it or dragged over it. You will find the two events in the Procedure drop-down list box in the code window for the form.

Let's plan a project to demonstrate the drag and drop event. The drag and drop event will deliver a letter into a letterbox.

Creating the human-computer interface (HCI)

1 Create two images to hold icons of letterboxes. Name one **PostBox** and the other **PostBoxFull**.

2 Set their two images to icons of letter boxes.

3 Create five images for letters: Set the **Picture** property to a letter icon.

4 Set their **DragMode** property to 1.

5 Create a label to document the form.

6 Make the **PostBoxFull** image invisible by setting its **Visible** property to **False**.

The icons for this project are supplied on the CD-ROM in the folder **Postie Pics**. The finished design of the form should look like Figure 3.77.

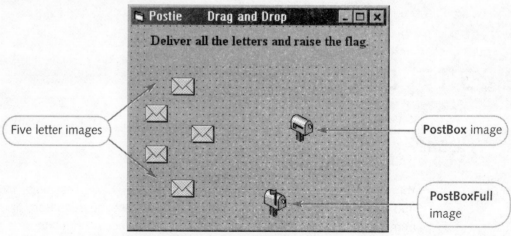

Figure 3.77 The design for the form

Writing the program

You will create a program to allow the user to drag pictures of letters into a letterbox. When all the pictures of letters have been dragged, the program will raise the flag on the letterbox image.

Plan for the event procedure *DragDrop*

1 Keep count of the number of letters delivered.

2 Set the dragged image's **Visible** property to **False**.

3 If the number of letters delivered (dragged) equals 5, then ...

4 ... set the **PostBox** picture icon to the **PostBoxFull** picture icon.

5 End if.

Code for the event procedure *DragDrop*

You will need to have the code window for the image's **DragDrop** event procedure open so that you can type the code below into it. Follow the step-by-step instructions that will show you how to get to the **DragDrop** event procedure for the **PostBox** image.

1 Double-click the image for the **PostBox**. Make sure it is the **PostBox** image and *not* the image for the **PostBoxFull** image. The click event procedure is displayed, which we don't want – as in the first part of Figure 3.78.

2 We want to get to the **DragDrop** event procedure, so click the pull-down menu of the event procedures available and select **DragDrop**, as in the second part of Figure 3.78. You can now type the **DragDrop** code into the code window that appears (Figure 3.79).

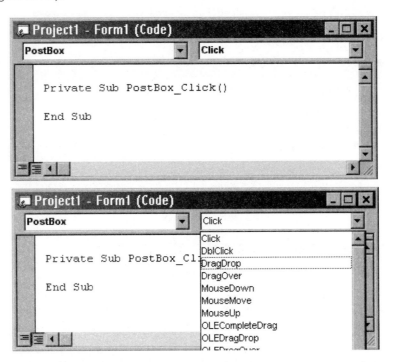

Figure 3.78 Revealing the event procedure pull-down menu

3 Type this code into the **PostBox_DragDrop** event procedure:

```
NumberOfLetters = NumberOfLetters + 1
Source.Visible = False
If NumberOfLetters = 5 Then
    PostBox.Picture = PostBoxFull.Picture
End If
```

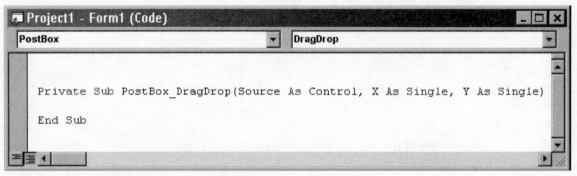

Figure 3.79 The **DragDrop** event procedure code window

4 In order to preserve the value of the variable **NumberOfLetters** on subsequent calls to the procedure, the keyword **Static** must be placed in the procedure declaration, as in Figure 3.80.

```
Private Static Sub PostBox_DragDrop(Source As Control, X As Single, Y As Single)

 NumberOfLetters = NumberOfLetters + 1

    Source.Visible = False
    If NumberOfLetters = 5 Then
        PostBox.Picture = PostBoxFull.Picture
    End If

End Sub
```

Figure 3.80 The **DragDrop** event procedure with the drag and drop code, and the keyword Static added

Running and testing the program

Run the program and make sure that only one of the postboxes is visible and that all five letters can be dragged to the letterbox. When all the letters have been dragged to the postbox, the postbox image with a raised flag should become visible as it takes the place of the other postbox image. This is demonstrated in the series of screenshots in Figure 3.81. Note the cursor's shape.

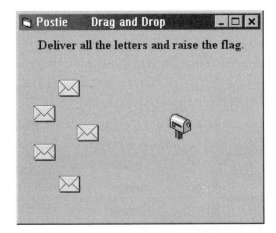 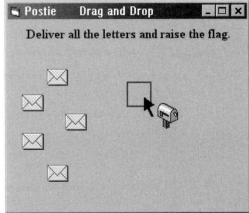

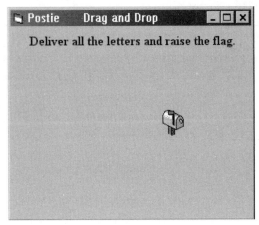

Figure 3.81 Testing the **Postie** program

Save your project as **Postie**.

 Now you try

Create a project that allows the user to place objects in a bin. When all the objects have been binned, a message should appear saying 'Thank you for keeping Britain tidy'.

Supertask

 Now you try

Design a program to allow young children to match letters with everyday objects like 'a' for apple. If the match is correct then a message 'Correct' should appear, otherwise 'Try again'. If the match is correct you should also ensure that the source (that is the dragged image) disappears. For each target object you will need to write **DragDrop** code in its **DragDrop** event procedure. You will find letter pictures A to Z in a folder called Drag&DropPicsforTask2 on your CD-ROM.

A quiz like the **Rivers Quiz** you created earlier could be modified to implement drag and drop for the user.

The source labels · The target labels

Figure 3.82 The Rivers Quiz adapted for drag and drop

In Figure 3.82, each of the **target labels** holds a **DragDrop** event procedure. For example, the USA target label holds this **DragDrop** event procedure:

```
Sub USA_DragDrop(Source As Control, X As Single, Y As Single)
    If TypeOf Source Is Label Then
            USA.Caption = Source.Caption
            USA.BackColor = &HFF0000
    End If
End Sub
```

If you want to investigate the rest of the code for this quiz program, and how the score is kept, you can find all the source code on the CD-ROM. The folder is **Drag&DropRiversQuiz**.

3.18 Internet Explorer object

The Internet and HTML: Visual Basic does the Web

HTML is the scripting language used to produce World Wide Web documents or pages. It stands for *HyperText Markup Language*. As well as allowing you to put text and graphics into Web documents, it also enables the linking of these pages which might be stored locally on your hard drive or anywhere in the world. A browser can then be used to view the HTML pages.

You can use the **Internet Explorer object** to display Web pages. You can control, from your program, what sites you visit and allow the users of your programs to link to the World Wide Web. Let's see how.

Adding the Internet Explorer object

Before you can display HTML documents in your program you must include the **Internet Explorer object** in your project. To do this carry out the following steps.

1 Start Visual Basic and open a new standard project.

2 On the **Project** menu, click the **References** command.

3 Scroll to the Microsoft Control (*shdocvw.dll*) reference, and then click the check box to the left of the reference name. Your dialogue box will look similar to Figure 3.83.

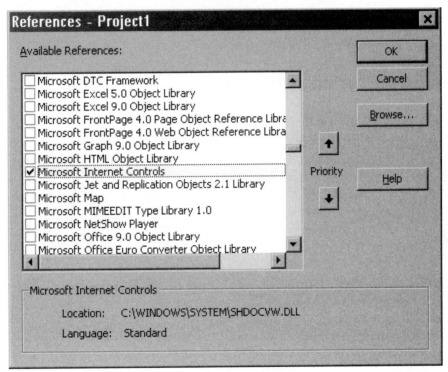

Figure 3.83 The **Reference** dialogue box with Microsoft Internet Controls checked

4 Click **OK** and Visual Basic will add the reference to your project.

The Internet Explorer object component has many properties and methods which can be used from program code.

Now that you have added the Internet Explorer object reference to your project you can write code to display Web pages.

Creating the human–computer interface (HCI)

1 Create a combo box for the user to select URLs.

2 Create a command button to call the **DisplayHTML** procedure.

3 Make the form and combo box wide enough to accommodate long Web addresses (URLs).

4 Set the form's caption to **Internet & HTML   Display HTML Documents**.

The form should look like Figure 3.84

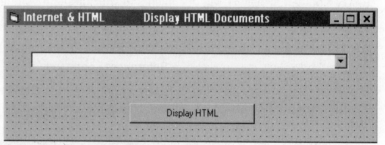

Figure 3.84 The design for the form

Writing the program

Using pseudocode to plan the program

In our planning of Visual Basic programs we have used English words and phrases. We have placed these words and phrases on separate lines to denote the sequence of events. To make the sequence clearer we have added numbers to the start of each line. This is called **pseudocode**.

Jargon buster

Pseudocode – 'Code' sequences written in plain English let us work away from the computer to plan the program without having to worry about the *syntax* of the computer language we are going to use. We use simple English sentences and phrases to describe what the program will be required to do. We will apply this method to the planning of our HTML program.

Plan for the program

1 Declare a variable for the current URL (address).

2 Fill the combo box with URLs at Startup.

3 Display the HTML document.

We will need to break down this plan further at step 2. How exactly are we going to fill the combo box? A good place to put the instructions to fill the combo box would be in the **Form_Load** procedure that, as you have learned, is carried out automatically when the program is first run. Here is the plan again with the extra steps included:

1 Declare a variable for the current URL (address).

2 Fill the combo box with URLs at Startup:

    2.1 Add the Microsoft home page to the combo box

    2.2 Add the Microsoft Press home page to the combo box

    2.3 Add the Microsoft Visual Basic programming page to the combo box

    2.4 Add the Fawcette Publication resources for Visual Basic programming to the combo box.

3 Display the HTML document.

Step 3 will also need to be broken down into more detailed steps. What instructions will actually be required to display the HTML document? There are in fact six steps to achieve this. Here they are included with the rest of the plan:

1 Declare a variable for the current URL (address).

2 Fill the combo box with URLs at Startup:

    2.1 Add the Microsoft home page to the combo box.

    2.2 Add the Microsoft Press home page to the combo box.

    2.3 Add the Microsoft Visual Basic programming page to the combo box.

    2.4 Add the Fawcette Publication resources for Visual Basic programming to the combo box.

3 Display the HTML document:

    3.1 Deal with unexpected errors when connecting to the Internet.

    3.2 Create a new **Explorer** object.

    3.3 Make the **Explorer** window visible.

    3.4 Open an HTML document corresponding to the user's selection in the **Combo1** box.

    3.5 Exit the procedure.

    3.6 Set message for the error handler.

Note that in this pseudocode we have used numbers to define the steps and we have added another level of numbering where a procedure will be required to carry out the task. Just by looking at the pseudocode we can see that we will need to create two procedures – the indentation and the second level of numbering makes this clear. One procedure will fill the combo box with the URLs and the other will display the HTML pages.

Code for variable declaration to hold a URL

The required code is:

```
Public Explorer As SHDocVw.InternetExplorer
```

Code for the procedure Form_Load

The required code is:

```
Combo1.AddItem "http://www.microsoft.com/"
Combo1.AddItem "http://mspress.microsoft.com/"
Combo1.AddItem "http://www.microsoft.com/vbasic/"
Combo1.AddItem "http://www.windx.com"
```

Code for the procedure *DisplayHTML*

Create a procedure DisplayHTML and type this code into it:

```
On Error GoTo errorhandler
Set Explorer = New SHDocVw.InternetExplorer
Explorer.Visible = True
Explorer.Navigate Combo1.Text
Exit Sub
errorhandler:
    MsgBox "Error displaying file", , Err.Description
```

The **On Error GoTo errorhandler** line will deal with any unforeseen error by jumping to **errorhandler:**, and will display the error message with a description of the error.

The **Explorer** object we created and set to show HTML documents will run Internet Explorer when the line **Explorer.Visible** is met. The **Navigate** method will try to find the page in the combo box in the line **Explorer.Navigate Combo1.Text** and display it.

Plan and code for the *Display HTML* button

The button will call the procedure DisplayHTML. The code is:

```
DisplayHTML
```

Running and testing the program

You do not need to have Internet Explorer open when you run the program, just ensure that your ISP has been dialled and you are on-line. If your school or college has access to the Internet on its network, just run the program.

Figure 3.85 An example of the program running

Run the program and select a URL from the combo box. If the URLs are not there make sure that you have included the **AddItem** methods to the combo box in the **Form_Load** procedure. When the URL has been selected in the combo box, click the button. The program should open Internet Explorer and display the Web page selected. Figure 3.85 shows a page displayed using the program.

Now you try

1 Add your own favourite websites to the program's combo box. How will this affect the steps that were constructed for the program? Describe to your teacher what exactly will need to be changed in the pseudocode.

2 Earlier you created a quiz program about capital cities. Why not give the users a chance to improve their knowledge of capital cities by supplying them with a URL where they can find out about countries and their capitals? Here is a useful website for that purpose to get you started:

http://www.worldatlas.com/webimage/countrys/sa.htm

Supply a button on the form that will display a list of similar sites. The user is then able to select one and the program will display it in Internet Explorer.

What did you learn?

Rivers Quiz program

If ... Then ... Else ... End If

- You learned how to use **If ... Then ... Else ... End If** to get the computer to make decisions.
- You created a quiz program about rivers to demonstrate this.
- You learned how to make controls invisible by setting the **Visible** property to False and how to make it visible again by setting the property to True.
- If you want to fill a list box with data at design time you set its **List** property to the list of data that you want by using the Properties window.
- You can allow the user to hide a password as it is being typed in by setting a text box's **PasswordChar** property to a character of your choice, normally *.

Finding the area

How to use parameters

- You found out how to declare and pass parameters to procedures. For example:

```
CalculateArea Length, Breadth, Area
Sub CalculateArea(ByVal Length, ByVal Breadth, Area)
    Area = Length * Breadth
End Sub
```

- Here the **Formal** parameters in the brackets are filled with the values passed to them and the procedure can use them for its calculation.
- We use the **ByVal** keyword to tell the procedure that the two variable parameters *Length* and *Breadth* have not to be passed back to the main program. This is known as **passing by value**.
- The parameter variable **Area,** however, has to be passed back to the main program with its new calculated value. This is known as **passing by reference**, so we don't put **ByVal** in front of it in the **Formal** parameter list. **Passing by reference** is the default in Visual Basic.

Using arrays (1) and (2)

More on list boxes

- An array allows you to group a list of similar data under one variable name. You can then refer to each item in the array by using the name and a subscript or index. With **Dim Cars(5)** an array is set up that can hold a list of five cars.
- An array is a special type of variable. An array allows you to group a list of similar data under one variable name. You can then refer to each item in the array by using the name and a subscript or index. The example **Cars( )** is an array.
- The **OrderWords Procedure** lets you sort a list of words. It takes two parameters (an array and a value): **Dim Cars(5) ... OrderWords Cars( ), 5**.
- You tried to use the **OrderNumbers Procedure** in the same way as the **OrderWords Procedure**. It lets you sort numbers in a list.

192

Learning to use Visual Basic

Diary

Connecting lists

- You met and used the procedures:
  TakeInWordsAndNumbers (TIWAN)
  OrderWordsAndNumbers (OWAN)
  OrderNumbersAndWords (ONAW)
  DisplayNamesAndNumbers (DNAN).
- These procedures take three parameters (two arrays and a value): **Dim Names(20),** **TelNums(20) As Integer** ... **TakeInWordsAndNumbers Names(), TelNums(), 5.**
- These procedures let you connect two lists so that when you sort one the other is also sorted accordingly.

Searching diary

Connected lists

- You met and used the procedures **SearchForWord** (SFW) and **SearchForNumber** (SFN).
- Help on how to use the Search Procedures.

Validating user input

IsNumeric function

You learned to check user input to make sure it is valid using the **IsNumeric** function. It checks to see that the user's input is a number. Here is an example:

```
Do
    SearchNumber = InputBox("Please enter a number to search.")
Loop Until IsNumeric(SearchNumber)
```

Grades

Select Case ... Case ... End Select

Using **Select Case ... Case ... End Select** simplifies the logic and length of the code. Here is an example:

```
Select Case mark
Case < 40
    Grade = "E"
Case 40 to 49
    Grade = "D"
Case 50 to 59
    Grade = "C"
Case 60 to 69
    Grade = "B"
Case 70 to 100
    Grade = "A"
End Select
```

Grand Prix

Select Case ... Case ... End Select

- The **Select ... Case** statement allows the computer to make decisions:

```
Select Case Combo1.Text
    Case "Ayrton Senna"
    GrandPrix.Text = "Ayrton Senna has started his lap"
Select Case Combo1.Text
    Case "Michael Andretti"
    GrandPrix.Text = "Michael Andretti has started his lap"
...
End Select
```

- You learned how to use a combo box. A combo box allows the user to select from a drop-down list or to add a value that is not already on the list.
- You can make a button's caption greyed by setting its **Enabled** property to False. This means that the user cannot click the button. This is useful when you want the user to click only certain buttons.

What's on the menu (Menu Editor)

- You can use **Menu Editor** in Visual Basic to place pull-down menus on a form.
- **Menu Editor** allows you to create pull-down menus with sub-menus.
- Selecting an option on a menu activates its click event to carry out an action.
- Adding menus to your programs can give them a professional look.

Lift (Do While ... Loop)

The **Do While ... Loop** provides a different way from the **Do ... Loop Until** to process a condition. Below you see an example of its use to process a password:

```
ID = InputBox("Please enter your password.")
Do While ID <> "Let me in"
    ID = InputBox("Please re-enter your password.")
Loop
    MsgBox "You have been given access."
```

- A **Do While ... Loop** tests a condition at the start of the loop so that it is possible that the loop is never entered.
- You used the **Do While ... Loop** to test for the maximum weight in a lift.

Café Bistro's pay-roll (Formatting output)

- You can format currency values with the **Format** function. If you want to format a value like 12.5 you can do it this way: **Format(12.5, "£#,00.00")**.
- The symbols for the **Format** function are: 0, #, decimal point, comma, -, +, $, (), space.

Dice (Rnd)

- To generate random numbers use the Rnd function. **6 * Rnd** will give you a random number 0 to 5 inclusive, fractions included. **6 * Rnd + 1** will give you a number 1 to 6 inclusive, fractions included. **Int(6 * Rnd) + 1** will give you a number 1 to 6 with no fractions, as the function **Int** returns a whole number rounded down.
- You used **Int(6 * Rnd) +1** to create a dice game "Double Your Money".
- You created *bitmaps* of dice faces to improve your HCI.
- You again used **Image1 = LoadPicture("Path to the picture file you want")** to place a picture in an image frame.

Using strings (Asc, Chr, Len)

- A string is any sequence of computer keyboard characters.
- A string must have " " quotation marks round it.
- You cannot do arithmetic with a string even though it may look like a number: "22" does not have a value 22 unless you use **Val**("22").

- So a string is made up of characters that the computer understands. The computer gives each character an ASCII code. ASCII is an acronym for American Standard Code for Information Interchange.
- For example 'A' has an ASCII code of 65, and the spacebar has an ASCII code of 32.
- The function **Asc** returns an ASCII code for any specified character. For example Asc("A") returns 65
- The function **Chr** returns an ASCII character for any specified ASCII code. For example Chr(65) returns 'A'.
- **Len** is a function that counts the number of characters in a string. **Len("Where is my hat?")** returns 16, not forgetting spaces and the question mark.
- You can use **Len** to find out how many characters a user has typed into a text box, with **Len(Text1.Text)**.
- You met the useful procedures **OnlyFirstLetter** (a function that returns only the first letter of a string) and **AllButFirstLetter** (a function that strips the first letter off of a string).
- You used the 'KeyPressedDemo' program to get the ASCII value for a character.
- You used the 'ASCIIDecoder' program to decode an ASCII message.
- You created a **CodeIt** procedure to create coded messages.
- You were given the task to create a project to decode coded messages.

Palindromes

(*Logical operator NOT*)

- A palindrome can be read backwards or forwards and have the same meaning, for example 'madam'.
- You created a program to test for palindromes.
- The logical operator **NOT** that inverts the logic of an expression was useful in testing for a palindrome:

```
If NOT(Pal = Word) Then
    MsgBox "That is not a palindrome"
End If
    MsgBox "Yes, that is a palindrome"
```

- You learned to use the function **StrReverse** to reverse the order of characters in a string. **Pal = StrReverse(Word)**, where Word is a string variable equal to 'ABC', would return 'CBA' and **Pal** would then be 'CBA'

User name and password

(*Logical operator AND*)

- The **AND** logical operator takes two inputs and returns True only if both inputs are True.
- **AND** can be used for example when an operating system is testing a password for a given username.

Input validation

(*Logical operator OR*)

The numerical characters lie in the range from ASCII code 48 to ASCII code 57. If a user when asked for their age enters a character with an ASCII code that is outside this range (>57 OR <48 … greater than 57 or less than 48) then the user will be asked to re-enter. OR is a logical operator that will allow you to test the validity of the codes entered.

Postie

Drag and drop

- In a drag and drop program you have **Source** objects and **Target** objects. The source object is the one that is dragged. The target object is the destination of the drag event.
- There are three tasks to create a drag and drop event in Visual Basic:
  – Enable drag and drop for the source object by setting its **DragMode** property to 1 in the Properties window or during runtime.
  – Select a drag icon for the source (optional).
  – Write drag and drop code for what happens at the target object in its **DragDrop** or **DragOver** event procedures.
- You created a program 'Postie' to deliver letters to a target letterbox and raised its flag with a **DragDrop** event procedure.
- You had the opportunity to improve the user-friendliness of the 'Rivers Quiz' program by implementing drag and drop.

The Internet and HTML

Pseudocode

- You can use the **Internet Explorer object** in your programs to allow your users access to HTML pages on the Web.
- You learned how to put a reference to the Internet Explorer object into your project.
- You were introduced to *pseudocode* and learned to structure it with special numbering that shows where a procedure is required to carry out a task. What you are trying to achieve is a line of pseudocode that can readily be put into Visual Basic. Take note of the numbering system to keep track of the level of detail.

Multiple forms

Load, show and hide forms

You got a chance to brush up your Portuguese!

- Projects can have more than one form. The commands to work with multiple forms were: **Add Form, Load Form2, Form2.Show,** and **Form2.Hide.**
- You went on to create a language tutor of your own choice with three forms.

File system objects

Drive, directory and file list boxes

- You used the file system objects to give·the user access to the contents of backing store devices.
- The drive list box allows the user to select a backing storage device on the computer system. You use its **Change** event to trigger a corresponding view in the directory list box. For example: **Dir1.Path = Drive1.Drive.**
- If the user double-clicks a folder in the directory list box, its **Change** event triggers a view of files for that folder in the file list box. For example: **File1.Path = Dir1.Path.**
- The file list box's click event allows the programmer to code for opening or loading files into the project. For example:

```
SelectedFile = File1.Path & "\" File1.FileName
Image1.Picture = LoadPicture(SelectedFile)
```

- You created a project that could browse the hard disk for picture files of several types (e.g. bitmaps).
- Help gave you a brief insight into error trapping by using **On Error** (e.g. **On Error GoTo errHandler1**).

Databases (display)

Displaying data

- Being able to work with external databases like Access can let you create your own customised HCIs.
- You used the **Northwind** database that comes with MS Office Professional.
- You learned how to use a data object control and set its properties: **DatabaseName**, **RecordSource** and **Connect**.
- Text boxes that will display data fields have to have their properties **DataField** and **DataSource** set appropriately.

Databases (find)

Finding data

- You used the **Recordset** object's properties and methods to find records.
- The **Index** property defines the database field for searching and sorting.
- The **Seek** method is used to search for the record(s).
- The **NoMatch** property is set to True if no record is found matching the **Seek** criteria.
- The **MoveFirst** method makes the first record in the database the current record.

Databases (adding)

Adding data

- You used the **AddNew** method to add a record to the **Northwind** database. **Products.RecordSet.AddNew** adds the record to the database.
- A text box with the data to be added gets the focus with **Text1.SetFocus**.
- A Help section gave information on the **AddNew** method.

Databases (delete)

Deleting data

- You used the **Delete** and **MoveNext** methods to delete a record from the database: **Products.RecordSet.Delete … Products.RecordSet.MoveNext**.
- A Help section gave information on the **Delete** and **MoveNext** methods.

Working with text files

Open, Line Input, EOF, Print, Close

- You can use the **Open** statement to open and save text files using the following syntax: **Open** *pathname* **For** *mode* **As** *#filenumberl*.
- **Line Input** gets a line of text from the open file.
- **EOF** is a variable marker which can either be True or False. It stands for **E**nd **O**f **F**ile.
- This section of code is an example of their use:

```
Do Until EOF(1)
    Line Input #1, LineOfText$
    AllText$ = AllText$ & LineOfText$ & LineWrap$
Loop
```

- The **Print** statement sends text to an open file. The **Close** statement closes an open file. This section of code is an example of their use: **Print #1, Text1.Text** or **Close #1**.
- The **Common Dialog** control has two useful methods to display the **Open** dialogue window and the **Save As...** dialogue window: **ShowOpen** and **ShowSave**. For example:

```
CommonDialog1.ShowOpen or
CommonDialog1.ShowSave
```

- The **CommonDialog1.Filter** statement allows the display of only certain types of file in the dialogue windows.

- CommonDialog1.FileName gives a path to a file. For example: Label1.Caption=CommonDialog1.FileName.
- You learned how to create an **executable** file so you can run your program outside Visual Basic.

Checkout

For Each ... Next, checkboxes, tag and controls collection

- You learned how to use a **For Each ... Next** loop to cycle through the controls on a form:

    For Each object **In Controls**
    Do something
    Do something else
    Next object.

- The **Tag** property can allow you to single out objects for special treatment or to exclude them from processing, as in the shopping trolley program.
- A checkbox has a default property called **Value** which can be set at runtime by the user to either **Checked** or **Unchecked**. The program code can then take the appropriate action on the basis of this value.

Using control arrays

Creating an array of objects

- Creating a control array allows you to treat a group of similar objects, for example several text boxes, as one unit or array. It is then possible to manipulate the individual values or properties within a loop just as you could with an ordinary array.
- You have to tell Visual Basic that you want a group of similar objects to be an array by giving each object the same name and by giving each object in the group a unique index.

Glossary

AddItem – When a control is created for the Toolbox, the developer decides what the control will be able to do and how it will be possible to use it. The control is given *methods* that can be applied to it by programmers like you and me. *AddItem* is a method that can be applied to a list box that allows an item to be added to it, for example **List1.AddItem "Shut that door!"**.

Boolean type – In Visual Basic we can set a variable to hold one of two values, **True** or **False**. We are telling Visual Basic that sometimes the variable might be true and at other times it might be false. The variable in fact takes on a **Boolean** type. It has a binary existence, sometimes worth a **1** (True) and at other times worth a **0** (False) just like in binary arithmetic. True and False are Visual Basic keywords.

All you have to do to make a variable Boolean is to set it either to True or to False. We need True and False in programming so that we can test conditions in coding.

Bugs and debugging – A bug is an error in the structure or detail of a program that causes the program to go wrong (*malfunction*) in some way. The term came about in the early days of computing, when real insects (bugs) would get caught in the internal wiring of computer logic circuits, causing the computer to malfunction and the programs to crash. Computer technicians would have to physically 'debug' the hardware by removing the winged or legged insects from inside the computer cabinet. There are two types of bugs or errors – **syntax** errors and **logic** errors.

ByVal – We use ByVal in front of a formal parameter to tell Visual Basic that we don't want the value of the parameter changed nor passed back to the program. What Visual Basic does, in fact, is send only a *copy* of the variable to the procedure and the copy can be destroyed when the procedure finishes.

ByRef – You can, if you want, put ByRef in front of a formal parameter when you are passing by reference. Visual Basic treats any parameter as being passed by reference *unless* ByVal is used.

Calling – Programmers talk about *calling* a procedure. This does not mean that the procedure is given a name but that Visual Basic is told to go and look for the procedure and carry out the instructions in it.

Clear – A method that can be applied to a list box to clear its contents at the start of runtime.

Code modules – A module is the Visual Basic term for a library of procedures or functions. A code module is used to store procedures or functions that are intended for reuse in one project or over a number of projects across multiple forms and modules. The procedures and functions in a module will be of a similar kind. For example you might create a module to hold just procedures that ask for numerical input and another module that has procedures that deal with text input. A code module when saved is saved with a **.bas** three-letter extension (e.g. Heights.bas).

Control – In Visual Basic the word *control* means the tool that is used to create the object on the form. It is not unusual for Visual Basic programmers to use the same term to describe the object as well. Controls in the Toolbox are actually programs to allow you to create objects.

Control variable – When you use a **For … Next** loop the control variable is the variable that comes after the **For** keyword. Whenever the loop loops, the control variable either increases in value (*increments*) or decreases in value (*decrements*).

Crosshair – The cursor that appears when you are using a control to draw an object on the form.

Debug – When a program is suspended with an error a window appears with options for you to end the program or to debug. If you choose to debug, the code window will be displayed, with the error highlighted. If you correct the error, you can either press **F5** to continue running the program or you can end the program by choosing **End** from the **Run** menu.

Event – An event (or an event procedure) is a set of instructions that can be carried out when an object on the form receives an action from the user. The action could be a mouse click for example.

Event-driven – A language that is *event-driven* means that processing is driven by events that the user initiates by actions like, for example, clicking on objects.

ListCount – The ListCount property gives you the number of the items in a filled list. Lists in Visual Basic are numbered from 0, so a list with six items would be numbered 0, 1, 2, 3, 4 and 5. To refer to the *last item*, therefore, the Visual Basic statement would be **List1Count -1**.

ListIndex – The ListIndex property gives you the number of the item that is currently highlighted in a list box.

Logic error – A logic error is an error that can go unnoticed because the program will seem to run all right but it will give incorrect results. Imagine you programmed a navigation system for a rocket to go to Mars and it arrived at Venus! The navigation system did not cause the rocket to crash, but the destination was wrong – a logic error!

Mid – The **Mid** function can pick out a character or another string in a given string. It takes three parameters. The first parameter is the string being dealt with. The second parameter is a variable or value that sets the position that will be the starting position to begin picking from. The third parameter is a variable or value that sets the length of the new string.

Naming of variables – A variable name can be up to 255 characters long, made up of letters, numbers and the underscore character.

- The name must start with a letter.
- There must be no spaces or other symbols in the name.
- Upper and lower case letters are treated as being the same.
- You must not use **reserved** words (names that Visual Basic uses for special purposes, like **If** or **Loop**).

Object Name Prefix – It is good programming practice to give the variables you use sensible and meaningful names, and when you use an object's name in code you should apply the same rule.

There is an agreed *standard of name prefixes* for objects in the Visual Basic Toolbox. The more common ones are:

- **cmd**   CommandButton
- **txt**   TextBox
- **lbl**   Label
- **lst**   ListBox
- **pic**   PictureBox.

Use a prefix for objects whenever you think it will help you to make your code more readable.

Operating system – A special program that allows the computer to be used. For example, Windows 2000 and XP are operating systems.

Path – A path is a set of directions that lets the operating system's filing system know where to find a file on the computer's hard drive or other backing store. For example, the code "c:\My Pictures\Icecream1.bmp" tells the filing system that the Icecream1.bmp file is in a folder called My Pictures on the C drive. Note that the path has to be typed in quotes. The colon after the drive letter and the backslash between folders and filename are also necessary for the syntax.

Procedures and Subs – Visual Basic has been developed from earlier versions of the language Basic, where **sub**routines was the name given to what we now call procedures. The keyword **Sub** for declaring a procedure was therefore kept for compatibility reasons.

Program – A set of instructions that is carried out by the computer's processor.

Project – Although the word *program* is usually adequate to describe what you are creating, because of the visual nature of Visual Basic the word *project* better describes all the components that a Visual Basic program contains.

Property – *Objects* in Visual Basic can be altered both in appearance and how they behave. To change an object's appearance and behaviour you have to set its properties. For example a *button* has a *caption* property.

Pseudocode – 'Code' sequences written in plain English let us work away from the computer to plan the program without having to worry about the *syntax* of the computer language we are going to use. We use simple English sentences and phrases to describe what the program will be required to do.

Private – The keyword that restricts the use of the procedure or function to the module in which it is created.

Public – The keyword Public that Visual Basic insists in placing in front of Sub in the declaration of a procedure or function has to do with where the procedure can be called from, or its scope.

Running – When applied to a computer program, *running* means that the processor is carrying out the instructions that have been written into the program at design time.

Standard.exe – This option allows you to create a program that you can later turn into an *executable file* that can run on any computer with Windows, without the need to have Visual Basic installed.

String – A string is a word or phrase made up of keyboard characters. For example, in Visual Basic you could create a string variable with a statement like this:

```
UserHobby = "Cycling"
```

In this example the variable is **UserHobby** and it has been set to hold the string "Cycling". The quotes around the string tells Visual Basic that we want the variable **UserHobby** to be treated as a string variable.

In a program using **InputBox** we could also set the **UserHobby** variable. For example:

```
UserHobby = InputBox("What is your hobby?")
```

Whatever input the user types in would be treated as a string and would be held in the **UserHobby** variable.

Syntax error – Errors that you make in typing instructions in Visual Basic are called syntax errors. If you make a mistake by, for example, misspelling a Visual Basic word the program will not run until you correct the error.

Variable – A variable is a single memory element that is given a name and that during the run time life of a program can be set to a value whenever the programmer requires it. The variable can have its value changed at various times depending on how it is used in the program.